# Walks Around The
# High Peak Trail

## The Walks

1. High Peak Junction, Bole Hill and Sough Lane
2. High Peak Junction, Cromford Canal and Cromford Mills
3. Black Rocks and Cromford
4. Black Rocks and Wirksworth
5. Middleton Top, Wirksworth and Carsington Water
6. Middleton Top and Bone Mill
7. Brassington, Carsington Pasture and Harboro' Rocks
8. Minninglow and Roystone Grange
9. Minninglow, Pikehall and Aleck Low
10. Friden, Pikehall and the Dales
11. Parsley Hay and Hartington Station
12. Sparklow, Flagg and Pomeroy

CURLEW PRESS

**Published by Curlew Press**
Derbyshire

Email: mail@curlewpress.co.uk

All rights reserved. No part of this publication may be reproduced, stored in a retrieval system or transmitted in any form or by any means, electronic, mechanical, photocopying, recording or otherwise without the prior permission of Curlew Press.

British Library Cataloguing in Publication Data: a catalogue record for this book is available from the British Library.

2nd Revised Edition

**ISBN:** 978-1-9161044-7-1

**Print** – Short Run Press Ltd., Exeter, England
**Text** – Karl Barton
**Walks** – Karl Barton
**Editor** – Louise Maskill
**Design and layout** – Mark Titterton

**Photographs** – Karl Barton – p.4, p.7 top, p.8, p.24 top. p.31 bottom, p.35, p.42, p.46 both, p.47, p.48, p.50, p.52, p.54, p.58 all

All other colour photography by Mark Titterton

**Archive Photographs** – Glynn Waite Collection – back cover. p.5 both, p.9 top, p.19 bottom, p.31 top, p.41, p.60 left

**Maps** – © OpenStreetMap Contributors (openstreetmap.org)
Contains OS data © Crown copyright and database right (2021)

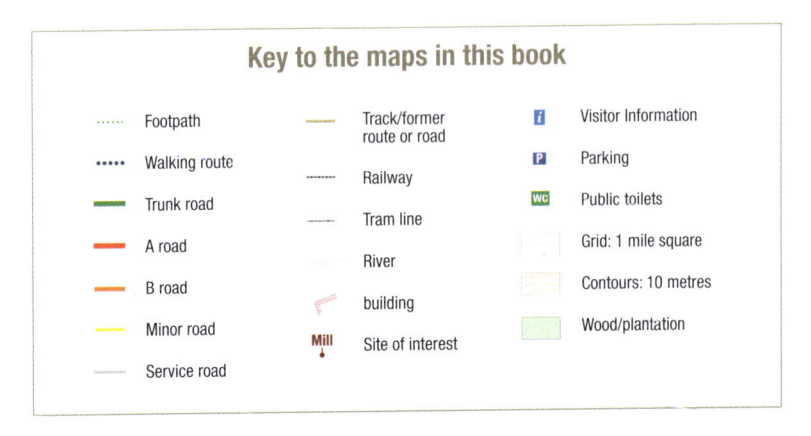

## Key to the maps in this book

- ......  Footpath
- •••••  Walking route
- ——  Trunk road
- ——  A road
- ——  B road
- ——  Minor road
- ——  Service road
- ——  Track/former route or road
- --------  Railway
- ——  Tram line
- River
- building
- Mill  Site of interest
- 🛈  Visitor Information
- 🅿  Parking
- WC  Public toilets
- Grid: 1 mile square
- Contours: 10 metres
- Wood/plantation

**Front cover:** The prominent landmark of Minninglow sits above Gotham limestone embankment
**Back cover:** Top of Middleton Incline

# Contents

Introduction ............................................................................................. 1
   Box: Inscribed Stones ................................................................... 7

Walk 1: High Peak Junction, Bole Hill and Sough Lane ............... 8

Walk 2: High Peak Junction, Cromford Canal and Cromford Mills ... 12

Walk 3: Black Rocks and Cromford .................................................. 18

Walk 4: Black Rocks and Wirksworth ............................................... 24
   Box: T'Owd man ............................................................................ 25

Walk 5: Middleton Top, Wirksworth and Carsington Water ........ 30

Walk 6: Middleton Top and Bone Mill ............................................. 38

Walk 7: Brassington, Carsington Pasture and Harboro' Rocks ...... 42

Walk 8: Minninglow and Roystone Grange ..................................... 48

Walk 9: Minninglow, Pikehall and Aleck Low ................................ 52

Walk 10: Friden, Pikehall and the Dales .......................................... 55
   Box: Long Dale Nature Reserve ................................................. 58

Walk 11: Parsley Hay and Hartington Station ................................. 59

Walk 12: Sparklow, Flagg and Pomeroy ........................................... 62

## About the walks

The walks in this book are suitable for the reasonably fit, ranging in distance between 4 and 6 miles. The routes will take you up and down some of the inclines on the High Peak Trail, as well as across fields and through woodland; sturdy walking boots and appropriate clothing are essential. Weather conditions can be checked online at www.metoffice.gov.uk. While the maps in this guide are accurate, they are intended to be used in conjunction with a detailed Ordnance Survey map, such as the OS Explorer OL 24 (1:25 000 scale) covering the White Peak area.

# Introduction

The High Peak Trail follows part of the former route of the Cromford and High Peak Railway, from the wharf alongside the Cromford Canal to just shy of the limestone works at Dowlow. The railway opened in the early 1830s and originally ran from Cromford to Whaley Bridge, carrying stone, minerals and coal from Derbyshire across the Pennines to the industrial heartlands of Manchester and beyond, and bringing back raw cotton for the textile mills of the Derwent Valley. The line boasted three tunnels, at Hopton, Newhaven and Burbage, and originally had nine inclines, each with a stationary steam haulage engine. In the early days wagons were pulled between the inclines by horsepower, but steam locomotives had taken over by the 1860s.

The railway was closed in stages during the 1960s, after traffic decreased steadily and the line became uneconomic to run. In 1971 part of the trackbed, a length of around 18 miles from Cromford to Dowlow, was bought by the Peak District National Park and Derbyshire County Council, restored and turned into the High Peak Trail. This traffic-free route is popular with walkers, cyclists and horse riders, and is part of the National Cycle Network as well as forming the first section of the Pennine Bridleway. It meets the Tissington Trail at Parsley Hay.

**Above:** The Puzzle Gardens, Wirksworth

INTRODUCTION

Hopton Incline

Cromford Goods – hanging on

The walks in this book all include sections of the High Peak Trail, but they will also take you further afield through some of the magnificent landscapes offered by the White Peak. Derbyshire's busy industrial past is belied by the now peaceful vistas, but human exploitation of the region's abundant natural resources over many centuries has shaped the environment and created some of the features we see today.

You will walk through Carsington Pasture, an area now dominated by wind turbines but where Neolithic inhabitants also left their mark, and look down on Carsington Reservoir, a thirty-year engineering project that opened in 1992 and is now a centre for conservation, sailing and birdwatching. The lead-mining town of Wirksworth is home to some of the ancient legal institutions that still govern the mining industry in the Peaks, while the village of Brassington also owes its existence to the lead miners who once burrowed deep beneath the fields and outcrops. Meanwhile, Cromford offers an insight into life in the textile mills, which brought the canal and railway to the Derwent Valley in the first place.

INTRODUCTION

## Inscribed Stones

A number of structures along the High Peak Trail bear commemorative stones. Those on the bridge at the bottom of the Hopton Incline are dedicated to the Right Honourable Lady Scarsdale and Emma Matilda Wilmot. Those on the Newhaven Tunnel commemorate the contractors who built the line.

**Above:** Inscribed stone with the crest of C & HPR, north face of the Newhaven Tunnel

A view from Harboro' Rocks with Carsington Pasture and the reservoir in the background

# Walk 1: High Peak Junction, Bole Hill and Sough Lane

## Essential Information

**Start:** Lea Wood Car Park, Lea Road, near Lea Bridge.

**Public Transport:** The TransPeak service between Buxton and Derby stops on the A6 adjacent to High Peak Junction.

**Facilities:** Cafe and toilets at High Peak Junction, at the start and end of the walk and at Black Rocks car park.

**Car Park:** Lea Wood car park, Lea Road (pay and display).

**Distance:** 4 miles

## About the Walk

From the once-busy industrial setting of High Peak Junction, the interface between the Cromford and High Peak Railway and the Cromford Canal, our walk takes us up the steep Cromford and Sheep Pasture inclines to Black Rocks. When the railway was in operation High Peak Junction was a mile away towards Whatstandwell; the location now known as High Peak Junction was variously known as Cromford Bottom and Sheep Pasture Bottom, since it was at the foot of the inclines.

**Above:** High Peak Junction

We pass a number of interesting features on the ascent to Black Rocks. Watch out for the incline catch pit, the site of the short-lived engine house at Cromford Top, a jib crane adjacent to an abandoned quarry, the engine house at Sheep Pasture Top, and some stunning views over quarries, Cromford and the Derwent Valley.

**Above:** Sheep Pasture Incline and (below) as it is today on the High Peak Trail

Black Rocks is a magnificent outcrop of black gritstone jutting out of the hillside. It is popular with climbers, and offers an interesting backdrop and viewing platform.

Climbing through woods, we skirt Barreledge Quarry beyond Black Rocks and ascend Bole Hill to its peak. Barreledge Quarry may have been a source of stone for St Mary's Church in Wirksworth and also for some of the mills and other buildings in Cromford. Bole Hill takes its name from the method of lead smelting once extensively practised in the area.

Descending over fields and through woods, we observe views over Wirksworth and the Ecclesbourne Valley. On the right-hand side of Sough Lane we pass one of the beehive-capped draw shafts of Meerbrook Sough. Work on the sough started in 1772 in order to provide additional drainage for mine workings in the Wirksworth and Cromford area, discharging the water into the River Derwent. The sough portal is dedicated to Francis Hurt, local landowner and proprietor of the sough at the beginning of its construction.

In 1777 an inscribed pig of lead of Roman origin was discovered on Cromford Moor.

## Directions

**1.** From the Lea Wood car park, take the footbridge over the River Derwent and the railway line to Cromford Canal. The track on your left, prior to the canal, once served a farm, later the Junction Inn before its demolition to make way for the Midland Railway, and finally served as an access lane to the now-disused sewerage works.

**2.** Cross the canal to the High Peak Junction visitor centre. The High Peak Trail starts its ascent between the rear of the visitor centre and the guards' vans. This is the area where the "hanger on" would attach upward-bound wagons to the wire rope with chains and leather straps.

**3.** Pass under the A6, and within a few yards you reach the site of the catch pit situated between the up and down running lines. It was the duty of the pointsman to hold over the points to allow safe passage of a descending train, their natural position leading into the catch pit.

**4.** After around a quarter of a mile you reach the site of the first winding engine for Cromford Incline, which was made obsolete by the introduction of stronger wire rope that allowed wagons to be hauled up the amalgamated Sheep Pasture Incline in one pull. The engine house was opposite the plate layers' cabin, which remains.

**5.** Atop Sheep Pasture Incline is the engine house. From here to Black Rocks the path is relatively flat, offering vistas over Cromford and the Derwent Valley. Passing Vic Edge's Bike Shed on your right, Black Rocks is around a third of a mile further along the trail. In the vicinity of a cutting prior to the visitor centre, a tramway once climbed the hillside to Barreledge Quarry above.

**6.** When you reach the Black Rocks visitor centre and car park, bear left off the High Peak Trail to take the footpath steeply upward towards Black Rocks. Keeping the rocks to your left, ascend into woodland, following the main path first left and then right as it rises up steps and follows the edge of a quarry and then towards the Bole Hill transmitter and triangulation point.

**7.** Beyond the triangulation point, continue through the gate and descend through woodland, over a stile, across fields and down steps to Oakerthorpe Road.

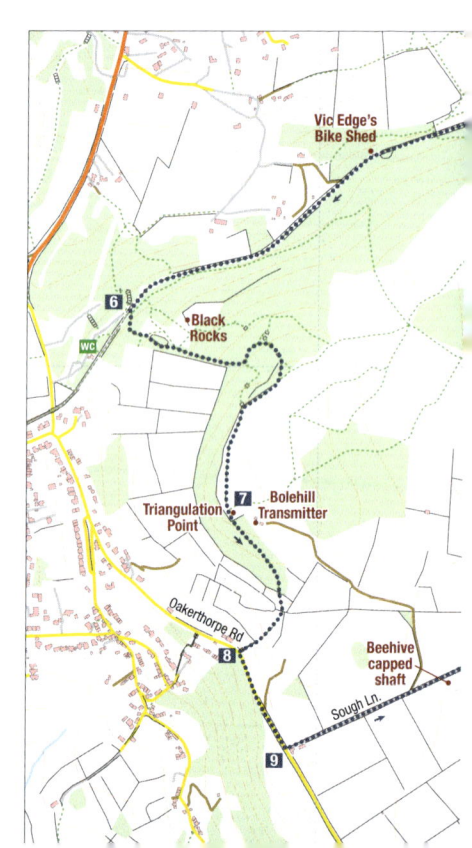

WALK 1: HIGH PEAK JUNCTION, BOLE HILL AND SOUGH LANE

**8.** Turn left up Oakerthorpe Road.

**9.** After 200 yards or so, turn left into Sough Lane (not named, but indicated by a bridleway sign on the opposite side of the road and with a low stone building on the corner). As you walk down the lane, notice on your right the beehive-capped shaft into Meerbrook Sough.

**10.** After about half a mile, past a farm and through a gate, continue ahead along a path where the lane veers to the left (marked by another bridleway sign).

**11.** Continue into fields, following the path for around a third of a mile.

**12.** Where the path turns into a lane, take the stile to the left of the gate and immediately turn left, crossing a small field and another stile to follow a path between field boundaries. The lane leads to the site of Meerbrook Mine and a farm beyond.

**13.** Cross Intake Lane and follow the main path through Birch Wood and over a stile to the A6.

**14.** Across the road and almost opposite the stile is a track which leads to a path down to Cromford Canal. Cross the busy A6 with care and take this path to arrive back at High Peak Junction, from where you retrace your steps to the car park.

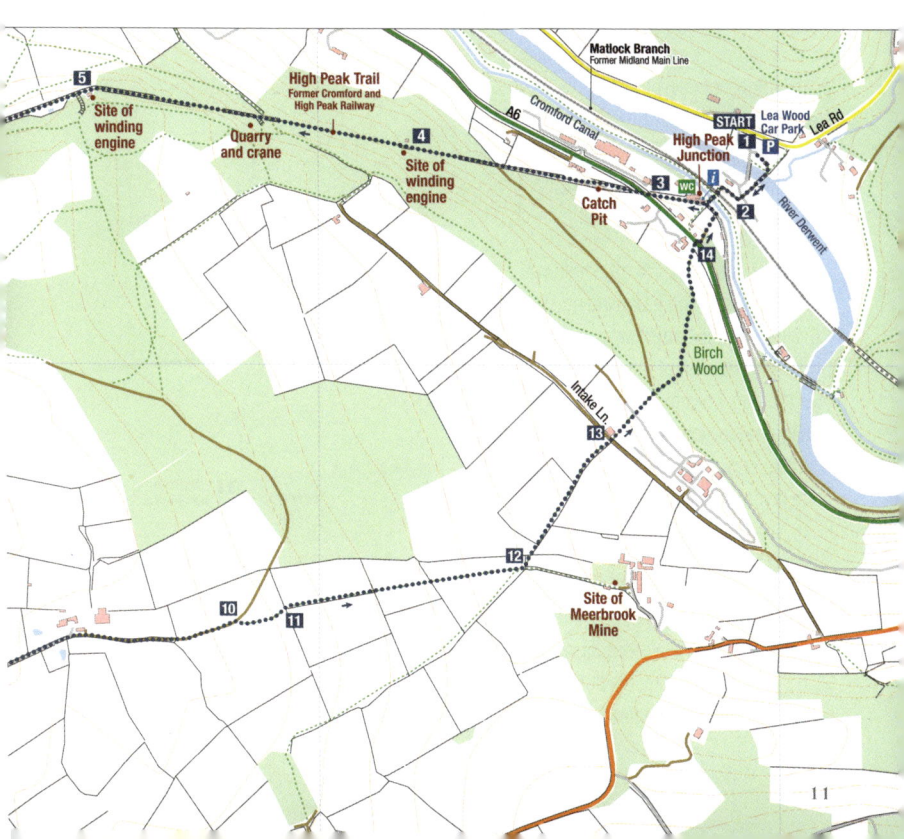

# Walk 2: High Peak Junction, Cromford Canal and Cromford Mills

## Essential Information

**Start:** Lea Wood Car Park, Lea Road, near Lea Bridge.

**Public Transport:** The closest bus stops are at Lea Cottages on Lea Road, services 140 and 141 operated by Littles and High Peak Junction on the A6 which is served by the TransPeak, operated by High Peak.
The closest national railway station is Cromford, which boasts an hourly service between Matlock, Derby and beyond.

**Facilities:** There is a visitor centre offering light refreshments at High Peak Junction, where toilets may also be found. Similar facilities are also at Black Rocks. Cromford Wharf and the mill complex offer cafés, shops and toilets Cromford village is a thriving community, providing a variety of shops, cafés and three pubs. Public toilets are provided at the Market Place.

**Car Park:** A pay and display car park for High Peak Junction is accessed from Lea Road, between Cromford and Lea Bridge.

**Distance:** 5 miles

## About the Walk

Starting at High Peak Junction, we make our way along the canal via Cromford Meadows to the wharf adjacent to Cromford Mills. Take some time to explore the mill complex, learning about its construction and operation and considering the thousands of employees who toiled within the confines of this once huge operation, before skirting the mill walls on our way to the village. Cromford's historic importance is emphasised by its inclusion as part of the Derwent Valley Mills World Heritage Site that stretches some fifteen miles down the valley to Derby.

Passing through Cromford's busy market place, we navigate the narrow back streets and paths and catch a glimpse of bygone infrastructure and ways of life, before walking up Cromford Hill and passing the Alms Houses. Dene Quarry, along with neighbouring quarries in the area, have been busy industrial sites for many years, employing large numbers of local people. This was also true of lead mining, the remains of which still pockmark the local hillsides and which once turned a rural scene into an industrial landscape. We join the High Peak Trail at Black Rocks, also once a site of industry, to descend Sheep Pasture Incline and return to High Peak Junction.

**Opposite page:** Cromford Mills

**Right top:** Cromford Canal **Middle:** The Gateway to Arkright's Mill **Bottom:** Alms Houses, Bedehouse Lane, Cromford

WALKS AROUND THE HIGH PEAK TRAIL

Lawn Bridge, Cromford Canal

## Directions

**1.** From the car park, take the footbridge over the River Derwent and the railway line to Cromford Canal.

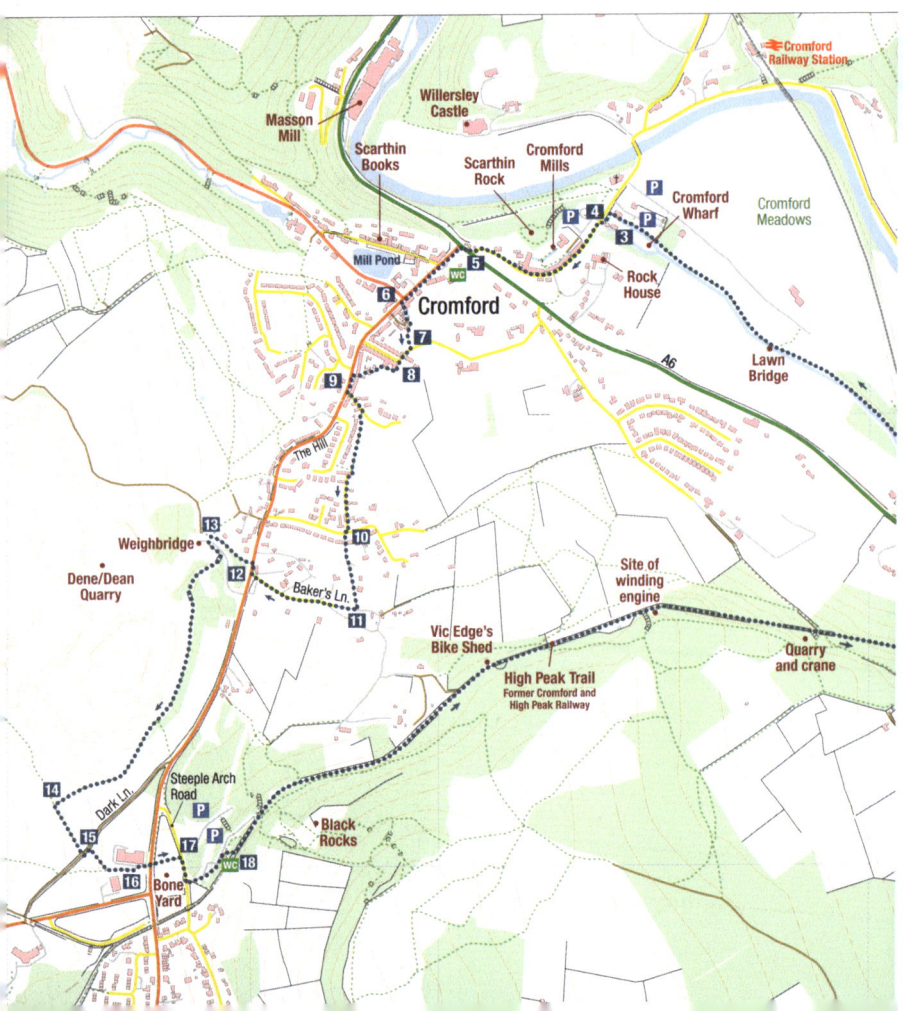

**2.** Do not cross the canal; instead, turn right and follow the towpath to Cromford Wharf. As you near the wharf, Cromford Meadows opens up on your right. The stream running between the canal and the River Derwent is a tail race from the mills. Pass under Lawn Bridge which incorporates a set of Brindley Gates, designed to seal the canal should a breach occur. Just prior to the wharf, on the left bank of the winding hole (a widening of the canal where boats could be turned) is what appears to be a tunnel. In fact this is the entrance to the private boat house for Rock House, only continuing for some 15 yards. Stepped access was provided from the house, which was once the home of Sir Richard Arkwright and his family. The leftmost of the two canal arms was a later addition to increase capacity at the wharf, being constructed around 1824.

**3.** Walk through the wharf buildings to reach the road, and then turn left towards Cromford village. The northern or Gothic Warehouse was constructed for the principal carrier on the canal, Nathaniel Wheatcroft.

**4.** If you wish to explore Cromford Mills, the complex can be accessed via the car park entrance on your right. Otherwise, follow Mill Lane to its junction with the A6, walking alongside the outer wall of Cromford Mills and passing the former site of an aqueduct over the road. The aqueduct was a Grade I listed structure that diverted water from the tail of Cromford Sough to power a wheel within the mill complex. Sadly the aqueduct was destroyed in 2002 when a lorry drove through it.

**5.** Cross the busy A6 using the pedestrian crossings at the crossroads, keeping to the left-hand pavement of the Market Place.

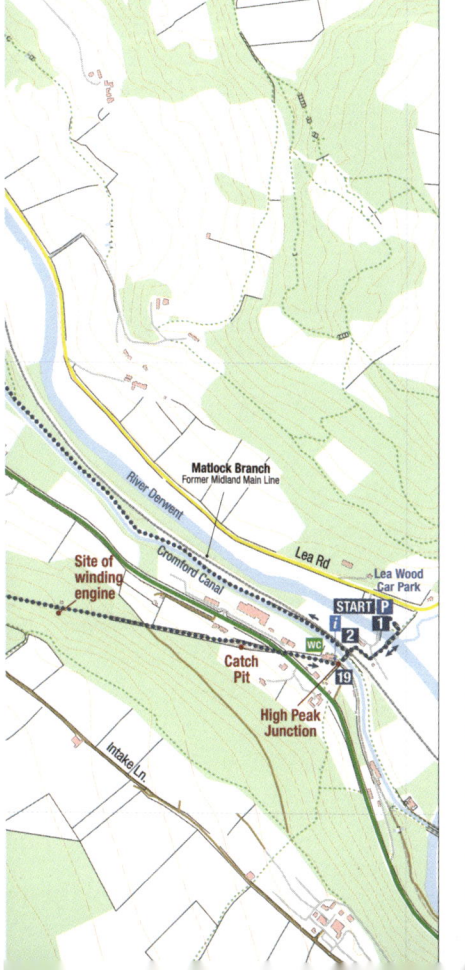

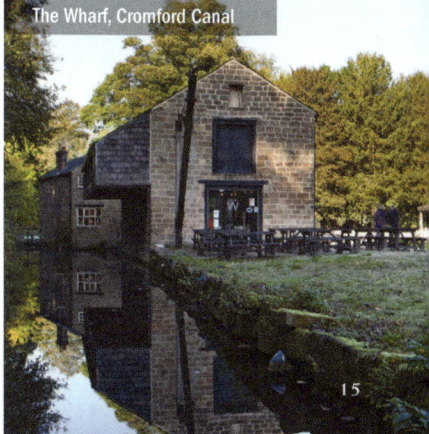

**6.** Just beyond and opposite Water Lane, between the buildings bearing the street signs 'Market Place' and 'The Hill', turn left and follow the path between houses and allotments towards the primary school. As you make your way around the rear of a number of houses you will find the Bear Pit. This is the exposed tail of Cromford Sough, which drained the lead mines in the hillside above and provided power to Arkwright's mill wheels. There are also a number of surviving pig sties in the area.

**7.** Turn right towards the cul-de-sac end of North Street.

**8.** Pass the school on your left and cross the end of North Street, taking the path opposite and following it as it meanders a short distance between buildings and allotments towards The Hill.

**9.** Turn left up The Hill (the main road) and then left into Bedehouse Lane. The lane forks right and becomes a path; beyond the Alms Houses, built in 1662, the path widens once again into a lane.

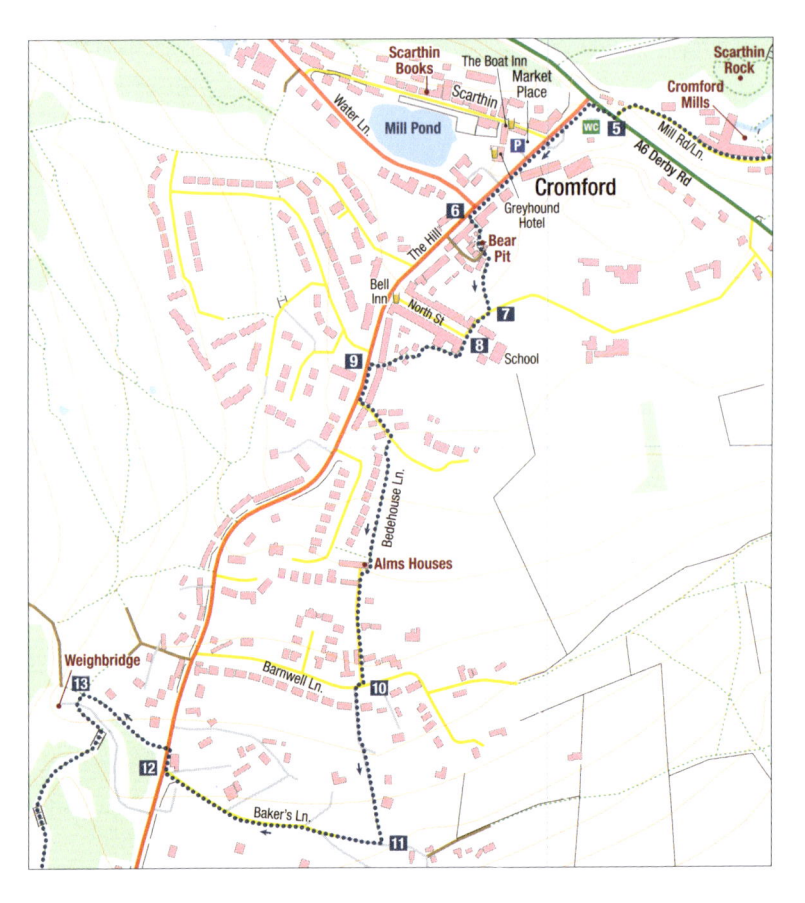

**Above left:** The Bear Pit, Cromford  **Above right:** Looking over rooftops towards Scarthin from the bottom of Bedehouse Lane, Cromford

**10.** Cross Barnwell Lane and follow the path to reach Baker's Lane.

**11.** Turn right onto Baker's Lane and walk back towards The Hill.

**12.** Cross The Hill and take the path almost opposite through a gate towards Dene Quarry.

**13.** With the weighbridges in front of you and the vehicle wash on your immediate left, turn left and back on yourself, crossing the quarry road and passing the vehicle wash again on your left. Beware the sprinklers that activate with vehicular traffic! Join a footpath a few yards ahead on your right (marked by a green sign), following it as it ascends steeply to overlook Dene (or Dean) Quarry on your right.

**14.** At the top of the path, at a T-junction, turn left and follow the path a short distance to Dark Lane.

**15.** Cross Dark Lane and descend to the industrial estate over fairly rough terrain, joining a path from your right as you do.

**16.** Walk through the yard of an industrial estate to The Hill. Cross and take the footpath opposite to Steeple Arch Road.

**17.** Turn right up Steeple Arch Road, and after only a few yards turn left into the car park entrance for Black Rocks and the High Peak Trail. Walk through the car park.

**18.** Turn left onto the trail, with Black Rocks on your right. After passing Vic Edge's Bike Shed the vistas open up for a short stretch before you reach the old engine house at the top of Sheep Pasture Incline. Remain on the trail and descend into the trees down the steep gradient, crossing Intake Lane and passing quarries and the site of the former engine house at the top of Cromford Incline. If you haven't "run away", avoid the catch pit in the trail and walk the final few yards back to High Peak Junction.

**19.** Cross the canal and retrace your steps back to the car park.

# Walk 3: Black Rocks and Cromford

## Essential Information

**Start:** Black Rocks Car Park, near Wirksworth, a signposted turn off Cromford Hill (B6053).

**Public Transport:** Rail: Cromford station, served by trains between Matlock, Derby and beyond, is around a mile from the route. Bus: Trent Barton 6.1, Hulleys 110 and 111, and the Transpeak in Cromford.

**Facilities:** Toilets: Black Rocks and Cromford Market Place. Shops and cafés in Cromford and at the National Stone Centre.

**Car Park:** Black Rocks pay and display.

**Distance:** 4 miles

## About the Walk

Our walk takes us from the distinctive Black Rocks, a natural gritstone outcrop, via some of the many paths and lanes off Cromford Hill into the historic Derwent Valley. Views of the mills and workers' houses contrast with the grand Willersley Castle and Riber Castle. Passing the site of St Mark's Church, demolished in 1970, we descend into Cromford, making our way around the mill pond.

While our starting point is now a pleasant rural location, this has not always been the case. The natural resources in this area have been exploited for many hundreds of years, and the current picture of serenity would once have been a hive of activity, noise and pollution. With a number of quarries, mines, smelters and brick works in the area, it would have looked, smelled and sounded completely different to the present day.

We pass the historic buildings of Cromford Market Place before turning up Scarthin, with its views over the mill pond, before descending back to Water Lane.

We follow Alabaster Lane up to the edge of Dene Quarry, crossing the Hopton Wood Stone Company branch of the Cromford and High Peak Railway and then continuing onward to the National Stone Centre. Passing the terminus of the Steeple Grange Light Railway, we return to Black Rocks along the High Peak Trail.

WALK 3: BLACK ROCKS AND CROMFORD

**Above:** Scarthin, Cromford
**Below:** Saddle Tank 47000 awaits the points to be changed at Steeple Grange

WALKS AROUND THE HIGH PEAK TRAIL

20

## Directions

**1.** From the shop and facilities block in Black Rocks car park, take the footpath down through woodland signposted to "Cromford 0.75ml." The area now occupied by the picnic site at Black Rocks was once the site of Cromfordmoor lead mine.

**2.** Skirt the fenced-off 'Black Rocks scree slope', keeping to its top side.

**3.** Descend over a stile into a field, and follow the wall line to a lane.

**4.** Turn left and follow the lane for around 300 yards as it meanders downhill towards Cromford.

**5.** Turn right through a stile onto a tarmacked path. Continue as the path becomes a lane.

**6.** Turn left into Barnwell Lane.

**7.** At The Hill, turn right and cross the busy road, descending The Hill. The three-storey houses almost opposite Barnwell Lane were built in the 1780s to accommodate workers from Arkwright's mills.

**8.** Take the path on your left, between 86 and 84 The Hill. The houses in the terrace starting at 86 were built in the 1780s, while those on the downhill side of the path, numbers 82 and 84, are of later construction, around the early 19th century. Follow the lower, right-hand fork and continue as the path reaches St Mark's Close.

The Hill, Cromford

**9.** Take the steps to the right of the lych gate.

**10.** Cross Hawthorne Drive and follow the path downhill.

**11.** At a t-junction, turn right along the footpath known as Alabaster Lane. At the end of the lane, on your left-hand side is The Old Cottage, some parts of which date to the 17th century. It is likely that the taller part of the building was raised by Arkwright in order to accommodate textile workers. On the opposite side of The Hill you will see a row of eight houses dating from the 1790s, two of which retain their 36-pane windows.

**12.** Reaching The Hill, turn left and descend to Water Lane, and cross to reach the Market Place.

**13.** Walk in front of the Greyhound Hotel, across the Market Place. The Greyhound Hotel dates from the late 1770s, and was used by the Arkwrights to conduct business. The rest of the buildings on this side of the Market Place, including the shambles (numbers 20–26), date from the 1790s.

**14.** Turn left into Scarthin, rising behind the row of shops. With the Boat Inn and the mill pond on your left, take a moment to look at the buildings on your right, the Post Office, a former chapel and Scarthin Books, perhaps calling in here for a browse. Follow Scarthin as it descends behind the former mill and Arkwright's machine shop to reach Water Lane.

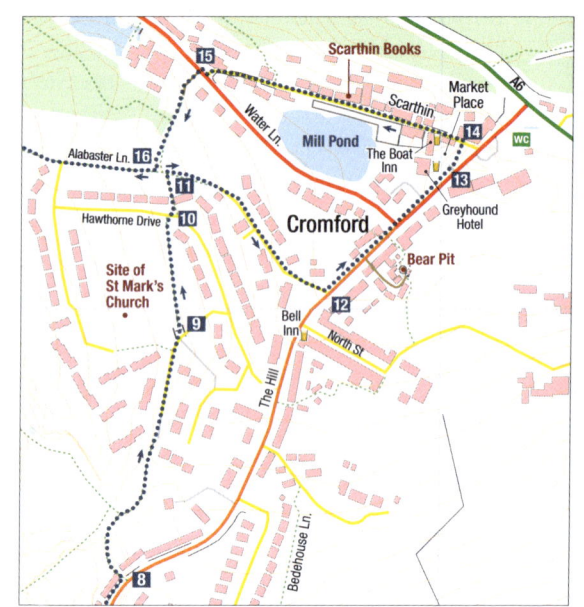

**15.** Cross Water Lane once more and take the footpath opposite, to the left of Walkers Garage, and climb back to Alabaster Lane.

**16.** At Alabaster Lane, where the paths cross, turn right, following the lane for around three quarters of a mile as it rises steeply to Dene Quarry. The surface of Alabaster Lane changes along its length from a metalled road to a grass track. Evidence of mining can be seen in the fields around the lane, some shafts being only feet away.

**17.** Cross the quarry road to the waymarked path opposite.

**18.** Follow the path around the perimeter of Dene Quarry for two thirds of a mile. The present-day expanse of Dene Quarry started to be exploited in the 1940s. The extraction of a quarter of a million tons of stone each year resulted in the void we see today. The area was once home to the Dragoneye lead vein, worked by Lath House, Dunrake and Chance mines. Primrose and California mines were also within the boundaries of today's Dene. Also swallowed up by quarrying were Yeats Lane, Baker's Lane and Longload Lane. The quarry's history predates the 1940s enterprise by over one hundred years, being noted as Denewood and producing marble in 1811.

**19.** Continue through woods until you see a stile above you and to the right; this leads towards Middleton. Do not take this path; instead, follow the path to your left and cross a stile to descend into the quarry. Since this area is an active part of Dene Quarry the location of the stile and path may move by some yards. However, the path will descend a short distance before crossing a level area and climbing back up.

**20.** At the top of the rise, turn right and continue for around 300 yards. The path initially follows the route of power lines and shares its left-hand boundary with agricultural buildings.

**21.** At a t-junction, turn left for a short distance and then take a path on your right, crossing a rough patch of land to reach a bridge over the Steeple Grange Light Railway. There are many paths across this heavily worked and uneven area, but the wall line to your right and the lane and railway bridge will shortly be within sight.

**22.** Take the bridge over the Steeple Grange Light Railway above Recreation Ground Halt, following the path to its junction with Porter Lane.

**23.** Turn left, crossing Porter Lane and immediately turning right for the National Stone Centre. There is a footpath a couple of yards to the right of the road, where the drive bends left and right. The dwelling on Porter Lane was formerly the toll house of the Ashbourne and Oakerthorpe Turnpike.

**24.** On reaching the car park, bear left and descend under the bridge, immediately turning left up the path to the High Peak Trail. The National Stone Centre's Visitor Centre is a little way further down the driveway, offering a café, shop and exhibition.

**25.** On the High Peak Trail, turn right towards Black Rocks and Cromford, passing the terminus of the Steeple Grange Light Railway on your way. The distance between the National Stone Centre and Black Rocks is a little under half a mile. After crossing Steeple Arch Road, the area ahead and to your right was variously occupied by Blackrock Brick and Tile Works and Venture lead mine.

# Walk 4: Black Rocks and Wirksworth

### Essential Information

**Start:** Black Rocks Car Park, near Wirksworth, a signposted turn off Cromford Hill (B6053).

**Public Transport:** Trent Barton 6.1 (the Sixes).

**Facilities:** Toilets at Black Rocks car park and Barmote Croft in Wirksworth. Café at Black Rocks car park. Pubs, cafés, and shops in Wirksworth.

**Car Park:** Black Rocks, Steeple Arch Road, Wirksworth.

**Distance:** 5 miles

## About the Walk

This walk takes us past the prominent natural gritstone outcrop known as Black Rocks, popular with climbers as well as for its magnificent views over the Derwent and Ecclesbourne Valleys, before continuing through the market town of Wirksworth and along the High Peak Trail.

Wirksworth is an historic market town, first documented in 835 and with a market charter granted in 1306. Its position and prosperity may be attributed to lead mining and smelting, and later to quarrying and textiles. The town contains many interesting buildings, with around one hundred listed by Historic England and some dating from the 16th century.

Like many Derbyshire towns and villages Wirksworth contains several churches and chapels, the largest being the Anglican church of St Mary. The Domesday survey of 1086 records the presence of a priest and church in Wirksworth, and the present building has been altered and added to over the centuries. In the churchyard can be found the 9-foot shaft of a medieval cross, although the head is missing. Venturing inside the church you will find T'Owd Man (see below).

The Midland Railway came to Wirksworth in 1867 and offered a passenger service towards Derby until 1947, after which the line primarily served quarries in the Wirksworth area. We cross the former goods yard and line to Ravenstor, a short distance north of Wirksworth station, via a stone footbridge that provides an excellent vantage point with views over the yard to the station. The Ecclesbourne Valley Railway has been running trains along the full length of the branch between Duffield and Wirksworth since 2011.

We join the High Peak Trail as it passes the former Intake Crossing, with Middleton Top with its engine house, wagon and signal a short distance further on. The final section of the walk takes in Middleton Incline, Middleton Bottom with its associated industrial archaeology, several former quarries, the National Stone Centre and the Steeple Grange Light Railway, which follows the former trackbed of the Hopton Wood Stone Quarry branch line towards Middleton.

T'Owd Man, St Mary's church, Wirksworth

## T'Owd Man

The ancient stone carving known as the T'Owd Man depicts a lead miner holding a pick over his shoulder and carrying a 'kibble' (a basket for transporting ore). The carving is thought to be the oldest depiction of a lead miner ever found, and it was removed during renovations of nearby Bonsall Church in the 1860s and brought to Wirksworth Church some years later. Now an emblem of Wirksworth, T'Owd Man remains there to this day, embedded in the fabric of an interior wall.

**Opposite page:** The gritstone outcrop known as Black Rocks

## Directions

**1.** From the car park at Black Rocks, follow the uphill footpath signed to Cromford Moor. Continue to ascend, keeping Black Rocks on your left. Skirting the quarry and bearing right, make your way uphill to the triangulation point and Bole Hill transmitter.

**2.** Go through the gate and continue into woodland and across fields down to Oakerthorpe Road.

**3.** Turn right onto Oakerthorpe Road.

**4.** After 100 yards, turn left onto a signposted path for Wirksworth and Bolehill. Pass the Primitive Methodist Chapel on your right, and note the signpost at the bottom of the path indicating the weight limit of 4 ton and exemptions.

**5.** At the crossroads with Little Bolehill, continue straight across, passing the Bolehill Institute on your right. Follow the lane and then path downhill.

**6.** Cross the Ecclesbourne Valley Railway via a stone bridge and proceed up Cemetery Lane to the junction with Cromford Road and North End. Why such a large structure over the valley, when a foot crossing over the railway would have sufficed? The farmer/landowner was rather insistent on a bridged crossing. There was also a clay pit, which the railway had severed from its direct route to the brick works.

**7.** Turn left onto North End, almost immediately crossing above where a tram line once ran under the road and into Barleycroft Quarry. After a few yards, opposite The Old Lock Up, turn right into Chapel Lane. Passing the Moot Hall and Temperance Hall, continue down Chapel

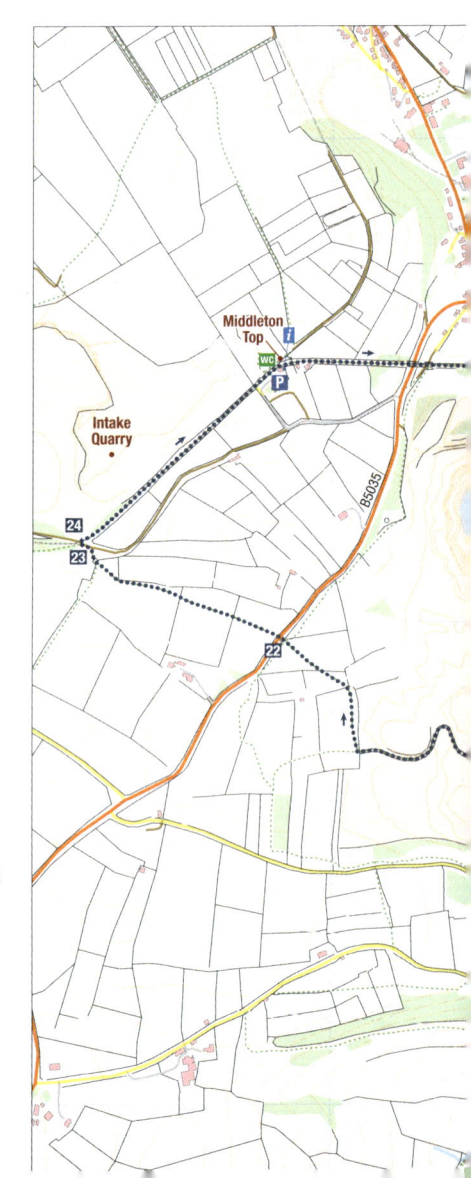

WALK 4: BLACK ROCKS AND WIRKSWORTH

Lane almost to its end. The Moot Hall was constructed in 1814 for the Barmote Court which, among other duties, settled the many lead mining disputes. The current building replaced an earlier structure. The Temperance Hall was constructed in 1860 and boasts a clock which, instead of the usual arrangement of numbers or numerals, reads "BE SOBER AND WISE".

**8.** Turn left around the end of the Temperance Hall and follow the lane down to Coldwell Street, where you turn left. The buildings you pass date from 1759.

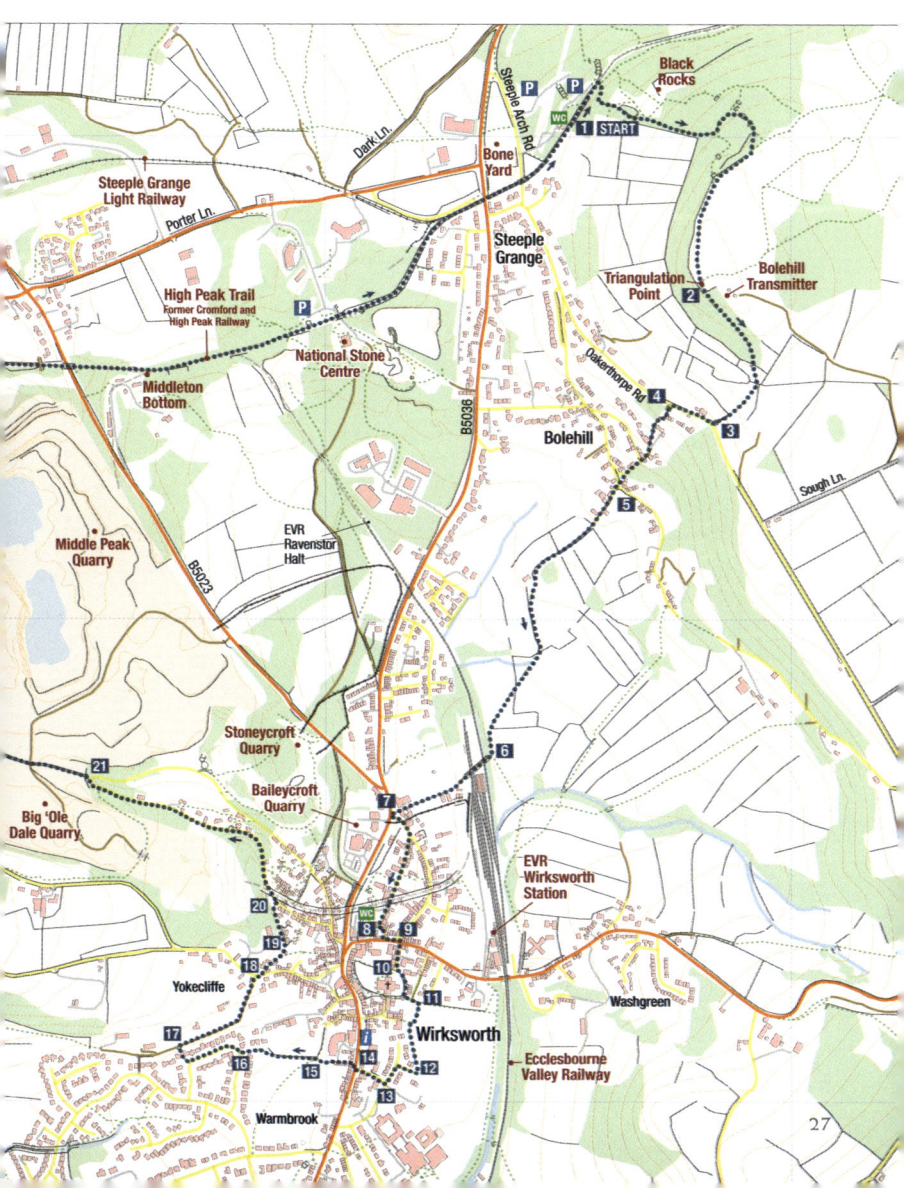

Moot Hall, Chapel Lane, Wirksworth

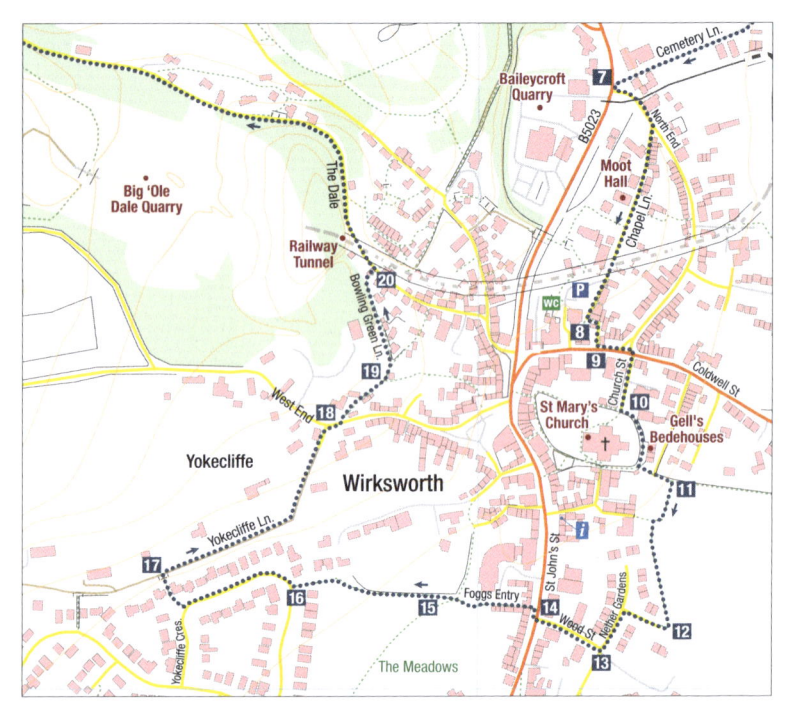

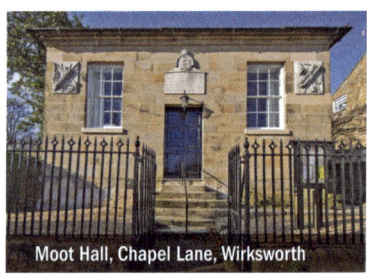

**9.** After a few yards, turn right into Church Street.

**10.** At the end of Church Street follow the path left around the church. Passing the old Grammar School and Gell's Bedehouses, which have been dated to 1584, take the first path left, heading away from the church and crossing the end of Blind Lane.

**11.** After a few yards take the path to the right, signposted for Nether Gardens.

**12.** On reaching the cul de sac of Nether Gardens, follow it to a t-junction and turn left.

**13.** Turn right into Wood Street.

**14.** Cross St John's Street and continue ahead into Foggs Entry, a narrow path between two houses.

**15.** Continue through The Meadows, keeping the high wall on your right.

**16.** Turn right into Yokecliffe Crescent. After a short distance, take the first footpath on your right.

WALK 4: BLACK ROCKS AND WIRKSWORTH

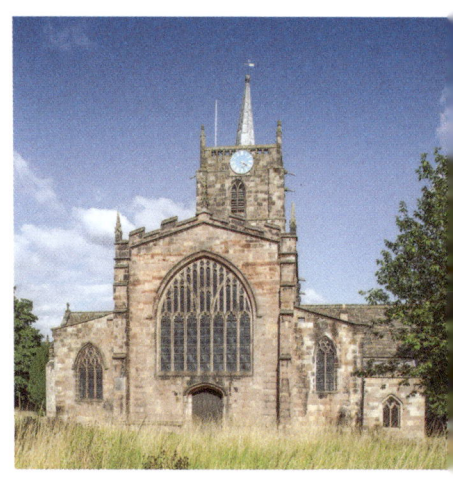

**Above left:** The Old Grammar School  **Above right:** St Mary's Church, Wirksworth

**17.** At the t-junction with Yokecliffe Lane, turn right towards West End.

**18.** Upon reaching West End, cross into Bowling Green Lane.

**19.** After a short distance, take the left-hand path.

**20.** Turn left onto The Dale and follow the lane uphill, passing the sites of two more chapels. Dale Quarry, also known as the Big 'Ole, is on your left; it was into this quarry that a tunnel was driven from the railway yard you crossed earlier. The tunnel opened in 1877 and ended the practice of craning stone from the quarry to a tramway, which made its way through town to the yard by the railway station.

**21.** At the end of The Dale, climb the steps ahead of you and pass through the clapper gate. Follow the path through Middle Peak Quarry, and then pass through a gate and turn right over fields to Rise End Lane.

Quarrying started at Middle Peak in the 1790s and finished in 1992, but mineral extraction is still permitted so intermittent working continues in order to preserve the right. Following mineral extraction in 1956 the adjacent Monkey Hole quarry was used as a test environment for tall structures, in particular the evaluation of electricity pylons for the National Grid. During the 1960s the site was subsumed by Middle Peak, leaving the landscape you see today.

**22.** Cross Rise End Lane (the B5035) and follow the path through fields.

**23.** Turn left for a matter of yards onto the lane for Intake Quarry.

**24.** At Intake Crossing, turn right onto the High Peak Trail. Follow the trail for a mile and a half, passing Middleton Top and descending the incline to Middleton Bottom, then continuing on to Black Rocks and the end of the walk.

# Walk 5: Middleton Top, Wirksworth and Carsington Water

### Essential Information

**Start:** Middleton Top, Middleton-by-Wirksworth, off the B5035.

**Public Transport:** Hulleys services 110 and 111 call at Middleton Top on their journey between Matlock and Ashbourne. Trent Barton 6.1, connecting Bakewell with Derby, serves Middleton-by-Wirksworth.

**Facilities:** Toilets and café at Middleton Top Visitor Centre. Toilets, shops, cafés and pubs in and around Wirksworth town centre.

**Car Park:** Middleton Top Visitor Centre.

**Distance:** 6 miles

## About the Walk

We commence our walk at Middleton Top, which provides an insight into the operation of the railway. The engine house contains the sole surviving working stationary engine along the route of the Cromford and High Peak Railway, which can be seen running several times a year. We descend the Middleton Incline, crossing a bridge over the old turnpike to Ashbourne, to the incline bottom where some of the old rope mechanism is still in

**Opposite page:** The engine House at Middleton Top

**Right:** Operating at the top of Middleton Incline

**Below:** Evidence in the landscape of old lead mining activity at Yokecliffe Rake Mines

situ. Descending the former industrial landscape above Wirksworth we pass what remains of the tramways that once served the quarries in this area. Negotiating the maze of steep paths and lanes known as the Puzzle Gardens, we cross Wirksworth to ascend to the scarred landscape of the former Yokecliffe Rake and the casts from numerous mines. With views over Carsington Water we skirt Stainsbro' Hall, before making our way to the shore of the reservoir. Turning towards Hopton, once home to the Gell family of industrialists, we pass many remains of the area's industrial heritage. We ascend the heavily-pitted pasture above Godfreyhole and cross the line of Tiremare Lane, an ancient route that is now just a mark on the landscape, before making our way back to the High Peak Trail via Intake Crossing.

**Note**: The current OS map OL24, which covers the Wirksworth area, is inaccurate. Some footpaths are shown as running through quarries and have not existed for many years, and others are inaccurately placed. Please use the accompanying map for this walk.

## Directions

**1.** From Middleton Top descend the Middleton Incline, following the High Peak Trail towards Cromford. We first cross a modern concrete bridge over the B5035, then the 1825 bridge crossing the old turnpike road. Within a cutting we pass under an old bridge that once carried a road connecting Wirksworth with Middleton. Middle Peak Quarry has obliterated much of this old route.

**2.** Immediately after crossing a bridge over Middleton Road, take the footpath on your right to descend to the road, where you turn left for a short distance. Before taking the path, however, it is worth exploring the area at the bottom of the incline. Just beyond a bridge over a track are the remains of wheel pits associated with the rope incline, now a scheduled monument. Looking towards Cromford you will see the remains of Greymare Mine and Coal Hills Quarry. To the right were sidings and the formation that was built to connect with the Midland Railway's Wirksworth Branch. Whether or not the track was ever laid remains open to debate, although contemporary maps would suggest so.

**3.** On Middleton Road, after only a few yards take the descending footpath on your left, and follow the path through a builder's yard and down the hill to Old Lane. Within the builder's yard you cross the formation of the sidings to Middlepeak Goods Yard and Quarry. On your descent, beyond Ravens Tor House you pass the

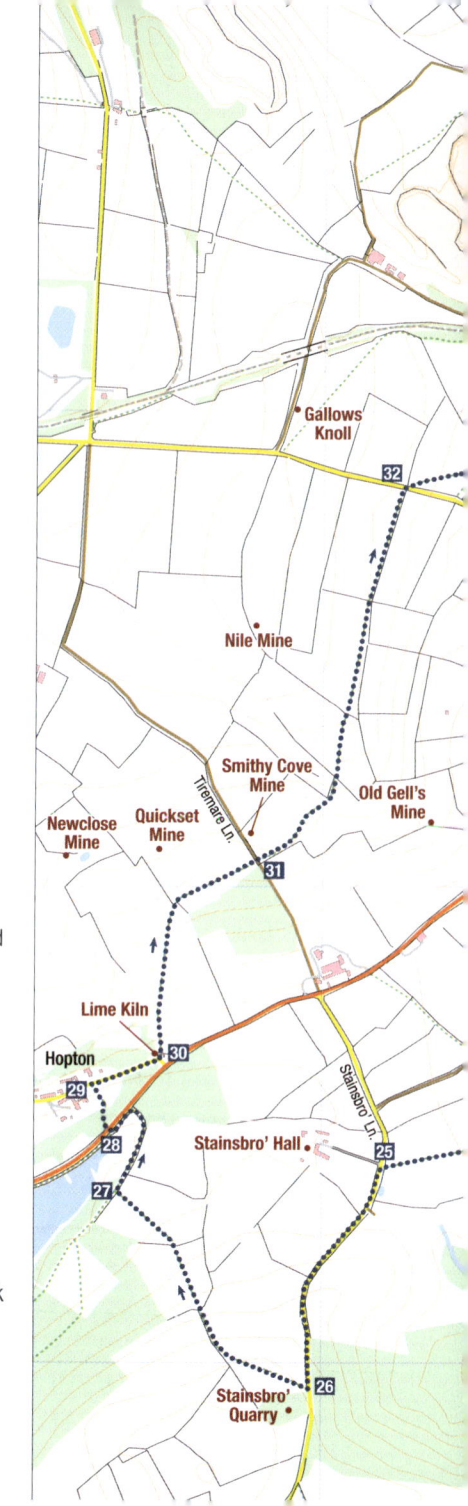

## Map Labels

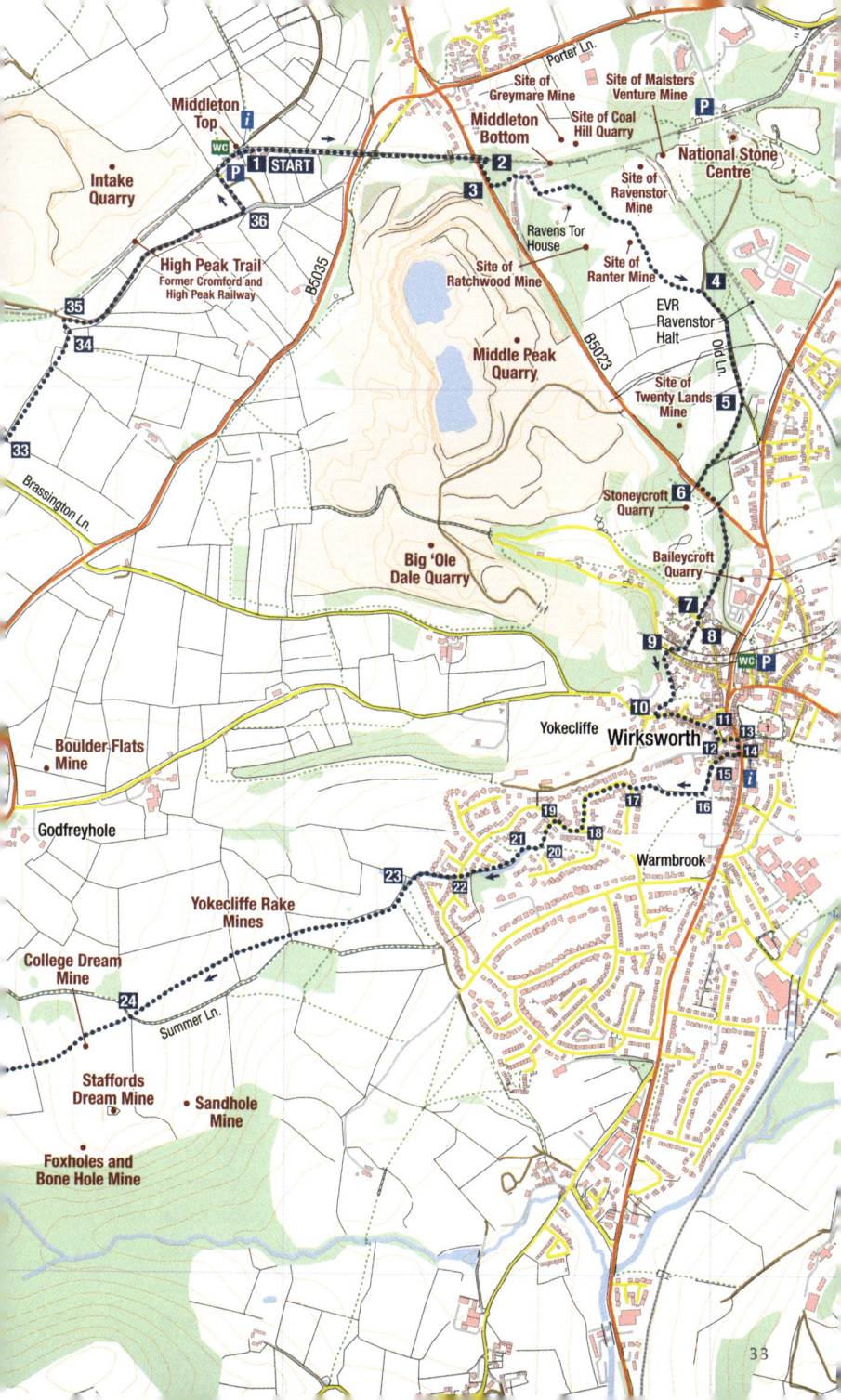

**Roads & Trails:**
- Porter Ln.
- B6035
- B5023
- Old Ln.
- Brassington Ln.
- Summer Ln.
- High Peak Trail — Former Cromford and High Peak Railway

**Locations:**
- Middleton Top (START, 1)
- Middleton Bottom (2, 3)
- Intake Quarry
- Site of Greymare Mine
- Site of Malsters Venture Mine
- Site of Coal Hill Quarry
- National Stone Centre
- Site of Ravenstor Mine
- Ravens Tor House
- Site of Ratchwood Mine
- Site of Ranter Mine
- EVR Ravenstor Halt (4)
- Middle Peak Quarry
- Site of Twenty Lands Mine (5)
- Stoneycroft Quarry (6)
- Baileycroft Quarry
- Big 'Ole Dale Quarry
- (7, 8, 9, 10, 11, 12, 13, 14, 15)
- Yokecliffe
- Wirksworth
- (16, 17, 18, 19, 20, 21, 22, 23)
- Warmbrook
- Boulder Flats Mine
- Godfreyhole
- Yokecliffe Rake Mines
- College Dream Mine (24)
- Staffords Dream Mine
- Sandhole Mine
- Foxholes and Bone Hole Mine
- (33, 34, 35, 36)

33

nearby remains of Ranter Mine and Ratchwood Mine a little further away, both on your right, while away on your left were the Ravenstor and Malsters Venture lead mines.

**4.** Turn right onto Old Lane. After around 150 yards you cross the point where a tramway passed beneath Old Road, connecting Middlepeak Quarries with the yard where the Ecclesbourne Valley Railway maintain their Ravenstor Station.

**5.** When just in sight of Cromford Road, turn right along a lane that shortly follows the former trackbed of a quarry tramway to reach Middleton Road. The tramway once crossed on the level into Stoney Wood Quarry. On your left you may see a cutting and bridge that once carried this tramway over another one that passed under Middleton Road to enter Stoney Wood Quarry. On your right are the remains of Twentylands Mine.

**6.** At Middleton Road, turn left, and take the steep footpath on your right just after the entrance to Stoney Wood, Wirksworth's Millennium community woodland. The path rises steeply to Greenhill between Stoneycroft and Baileycroft quarries, offering views over the town to the left and the community woodland to the right.

**7.** Turn left down Greenhill for a few yards. The large building ahead and below is Babington House, built around 1630, not in 1588 as the date on the more modern porch suggests. The building was once Wirksworth's hospital.

**8.** Turn right along a path with handrails set into the wall. Continue along this path through the area known as the Puzzle Gardens, enjoying the views over the rooftops of Wirksworth. Pass over the railway tunnel and descend to The Dale, which may once have formed part of the Portway, an ancient trackway that ran from the Nottingham area to Mam Tor.

**9.** Turn left and immediately right up the path named Bowling Green Lane, following it to reach West End (ignore paths off to the left).

**10.** Turn left to descend West End to the Market Place with its array of private dwellings, shops and pubs. Take your time to explore this interesting area of town, before returning to the car park that now occupies the Market Place.

**11.** Pass behind the Hope and Anchor pub to descend to The Causeway.

**12.** Turn left into The Causeway, continuing for a few yards to St John's Street.

**13.** Turn right into St John's Street for a few yards to the junction with Hammond Court, opposite which may be seen the outline and former site of a timber-framed, cruck truss building near Wirksworth Heritage Centre.

**14.** Turn right into Hammond Court, following it down to the left where it becomes a path.

**15.** Follow the path between walls to The Meadows.

**Above:** Overlooking the rooftops from the Puzzle Gardens in Wirksworth

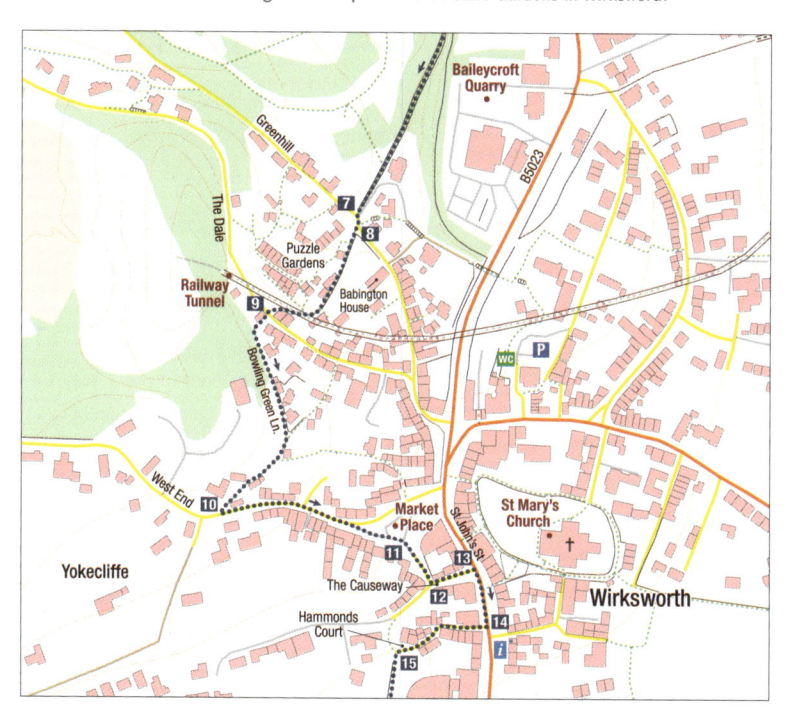

35

*The Market Place, Wirksworth*

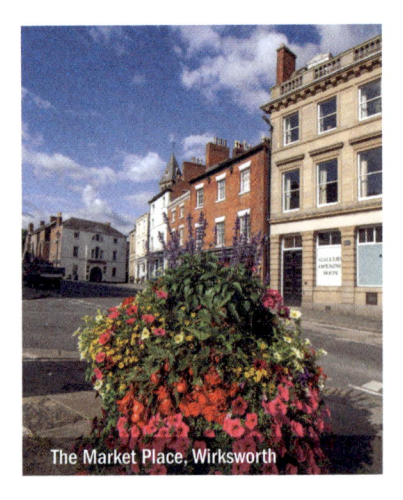

**16.** Turn right across The Meadows, keeping the high wall to your right.

**17.** Turn right into Yokecliffe Crescent, following it round to Yokecliffe Drive.

**18.** Turn right into Yokecliffe Drive for around 50 yards.

**19.** Take the first road to the left, also Yokecliffe Drive. A public footpath bears left from the end of the road, which you should follow.

**20.** Keep to the right-hand paths until you reach a children's play area.

**21.** Take the left-hand path past the play area.

**22.** Cross Yokecliffe Drive and continue along the path.

**23.** Keeping to the right-hand path, walk up the hill through the area of Yokecliffe Rake Mines. Yokecliffe Mine itself was some way off to your right.

**24.** Cross Summer Lane, following the path towards Stainsbro' Hall. To your left were the Stafford's Dream, College Dream, Foxholes, Bone Hole and Sandhole mines.

**25.** At Stainsbro' Lane, turn left and walk up the hill in the direction of Callow and Kirk Ireton.

**26.** After around a third of a mile, take the footpath on your right and maintain your direction to descend across several fields towards Carsington Water. Stainsbro' Quarry is immediately to your left after leaving Stainsbro' Lane.

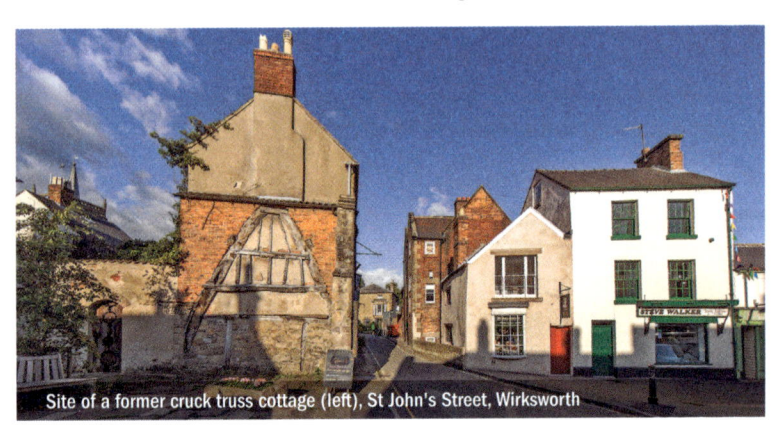

*Site of a former cruck truss cottage (left), St John's Street, Wirksworth*

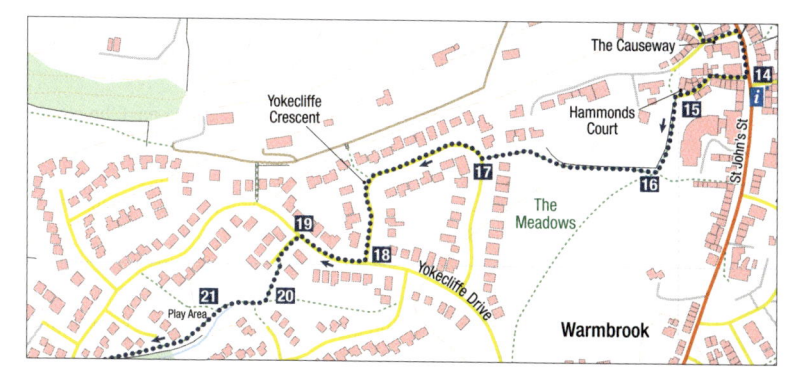

**27.** Turn right onto the wide trail that encircles Carsington Water, continuing for around 250 yards.

**28.** After the sharp left turn in the trail, take the path on your right marked 'Hopton', cross the busy B5035 and follow the path ahead.

**29.** At the Hopton road, with the 18th century house Woodbank in front of you, turn right away from the village and pass the remains of a lime kiln on your left.

**30.** At the junction of the Hopton road and the B5035, take the footpath on your left. Ascend the field, passing to the left of the central clump of trees; the remains of Old Jacob's, Newclose and Quickset mines are on your left, along with other shafts dotted around the landscape.

**31.** Beyond what remains of Tiremare Lane, continue across a field containing numerous abandoned lead mines of the Yokecliffe Rake. Tiremare Lane is no longer a public right of way, being severed at its junctions with both Stainsbro' Lane and Brassington Lane. Immediately on your left at Tiremare Lane was Smithycove lead mine. Crossing the distinct line of mine workings in the next field, Oldgell's Mine is on your right. Closer to Brassington Lane, Nile Mine is a short distance away to your left. Nile Mine was peculiar, having hand- and footholds cut into the shaft, rather than the more usual stemples (wooden beams) fixed into the shaft for climbing.

**32.** Cross Brassington Lane, and descend across the next field to a wall. This section of Brassington Lane may also once have formed part of the Portway.

**33.** Cross the ladder stile over the wall and turn left, following the field boundary on your left as it rises.

**34.** Where a path joins from the right, turn left through a stile to ascend steeply to a lane.

**35.** Turn right onto the lane for around a third of a mile. On your left is the High Peak Trail, which crosses a bridge that provided access to the land between the former railway and Intake Quarry.

**36.** Turn left to return to Middleton Top.

# Walk 6: Middleton Top and Bone Mill

## Essential Information

**Start:** Middleton Top, Middleton-by-Wirksworth, off the B5035.

**Public Transport:** Hulleys services 110 and 111 call at Middleton Top on their journey between Matlock and Ashbourne. Trent Barton 6.1, connecting Bakewell with Derby, serves Middleton-by-Wirksworth.

**Facilities:** Toilets and café at Middleton Top Visitor Centre. Refreshments at the Nelson Arms pub in Middleton.

**Car Park:** Middleton Top Visitor Centre.

**Distance:** 5 miles

## About the Walk

Middleton Top is the location of one of the stationary winding engines that once served the Cromford and High Peak Railway (C&HPR). The engine has been preserved and operates some weekends between April and October; please see Derbyshire County Council's website for details.

Our walk starts by crossing one of the former quarry branch lines before ascending Middleton Moor, under which are many miles of tunnels dug during the extraction

Engine House, Middleton Top

of minerals and ore, particularly lead. A collapse in the 1980s has left a noticeable depression to the eastern side of the moor. We pass the mysterious 'fence test site' before descending to the outskirts of Middleton. Climbing out of the village we pass several derelict buildings and lots more evidence of lead mining.

Descending to Hoptonwood Quarries we pass close to one of the entrances to the aforementioned tunnel system. Hoptonwood Quarries was served by another branch of the C&HPR, and its embankment and bridge can be seen beyond the farmyard near the start of our ascent towards Griffe Grange.

WALK 6: MIDDLETON TOP AND BONE MILL

Skirting Bonemill Quarry, now known as Ryder Point with its three wind turbines, we make our way to the highest point of the walk before descending to Hopton Top and the former site of the steepest adhesion railway in Britain, with a gradient of 1 in 14. Beyond Hopton Bottom are the remains of the Hopton Wood winding engine, which was last used around 1877. Before returning to Middleton Top we pass through the 113-yard Hopton Tunnel.

## Directions

**1.** Take the footpath opposite the cycle hire centre, signposted Middleton Moor. The earthworks here are the remains of a narrow gauge tramway that once served the quarries above Middleton. Bear left to follow the track uphill and across fields for around a third of a mile. This now open area was once subdivided into many enclosures and crossed by Samuel Lane; Samuel lead mine was on your left, just over half-way between Middleton Top and Rains's Lane (sic).

**2.** Facing the fence testing site, turn right to descend Rains's Lane (sic) for a short distance, enjoying the views over Middleton, Matlock and beyond.

**3.** Turn left onto The Moor; a mineral railway once ran along part of this lane to a former quarry on the left. We crossed the start of the siding at Middleton Top. Follow the lane a short distance to Water Lane.

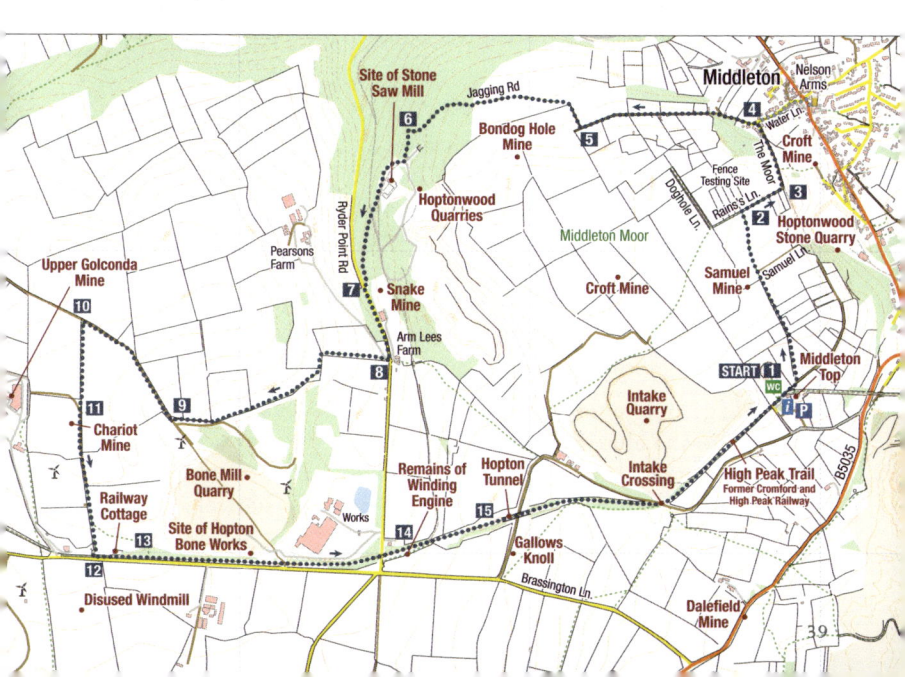

**4.** At the junction of The Moor and Water Lane, if refreshments are required, turn right down the hill and you will find the Nelson Arms pub. Otherwise, turn left and follow the lane uphill for around a third of a mile.

**5.** Just before the end of the lane and marked by a yellow waypoint arrow, turn right to follow the path (the old Middleton to Hopton Jagging Road) between the spoil heaps from long-disused mines. Because of the terrain and vegetation cover the path may be difficult to follow, but it continues for around half a mile, crossing the undulating landscape before skirting a quarry edge. This area is a scheduled monument containing the remains of Black Rakes, Welshmans Venture Mine, Bondog Hole Mine and Merry Tom and Thumper Sitch Levels.

**6.** Descend to the floor of the disused Hoptonwood Quarries. The area before you was once a stone saw mill. On your left is the entrance to mine workings through to Middleton. Turn right to follow the roadway down to the road joining Hopton to the busy Via Gellia road. Hoptonwood quarries were served by sidings from the Cromford and High Peak Railway, the junction to which we will pass later. To the left of the road junction was Snake Mine, its shaft descending some 250 feet. There is photographic evidence of a standing, but ruined, horse gin dating from 1913.

**7.** Turn left and walk up Ryder Point Road for less than 300 yards to Arm Lees Farm on your left. Behind the farm is a bridge through the embankment carrying the sidings to the quarries.

**8.** Immediately after the track for Pearsons Farm, take the path on the right and ascend the hill, crossing stiles and fields and following yellow waypoint arrows towards the wind turbines in Bonemill Quarry.

**9.** Where the path meets a track, turn right in the direction of New Harborough Farm (ignore a footpath to the left). This wide track may once have formed part of the Portway, an ancient trackway connecting the Hope Valley to the lower Derwent and beyond.

Former railway cottage at Hopton Top

LNWR 2-4-0t 3049 atop Hopton Incline with a "Fly" passenger coach at the rear of the formation (Early 1890s)

10. Less than 200 yards beyond a slight left-hand turn in the track, turn left at the signpost for High Peak Trail and Hopton Top.

11. Passing several mounds and a water tank at the site of Chariot Mine, follow the path down to the High Peak Trail. To the right of Chariot Mine is the site of Upper Golconda Mine. The mine's coe (a hut or small stone building at the top of a mineshaft, intended to protect miners from the weather as they emerged from underground) is said to survive within one of the industrial units.

12. At the High Peak Trail turn left, passing the railway cottage that was last inhabited by Thurston Matkin and family, before the railway closed and the building passed into the hands of Derbyshire County Council.

13. Descend Hopton Incline with Bone Mill Quarry on your left and continue along the trail, crossing two tall bridges, the first leading directly into the quarry and the second straddling the Hopton to Via Gellia road (look to your left to see Arm Lees Farm, passed earlier in the walk). Bone Mill Quarry presumably took its name from the Hopton Bone Works that once stood in the area.

14. Beyond the second bridge are the partial remains of a stationary engine, down the embankment to your right. An engine house was erected here in 1856 to provide power to haul wagons up the branch from Hoptonwood Quarries. Originally the engine and its house would have been at track level, but Hopton Incline was rebuilt in 1877 and the now-disused engine was left to rot in situ. The branch to the quarries can be seen crossing the fields to your left.

15. Continue along the trail through the 113-yard Hopton Tunnel, before passing the site of Intake Crossing and returning to Middleton Top.

# Walk 7: Brassington, Carsington Pasture and Harboro' Rocks

## Essential Information

**Start:** Wirksworth Dale Car Park, off Dale End, Brassington.

**Public Transport:** Hulleys bus service 411, operates between Ashbourne and Matlock.

**Facilities:** Brassington: Pubs, Ye Olde Gate Inn and The Miner's Arms. Carsington: Pub, The Miner's Arms.

**Car Park:** Wirksworth Dale, Brassington. Small, remote and free.

**Distance:** 5½ miles

**Note:** Some of this walk uses public roads with no footway.
This is a former lead-mining area. While the deep mines have been capped, it is not a good idea to wander into the many workings that litter the landscape. Timber caps may have rotted and earth shifted over the decades; who knows what may lie beneath the seemingly benign shallow pits.
Many stiles in Derbyshire are formed of two vertical stone stoops. These are generally classified as squeezer stiles, although locally they are known as 'fat man's miseries'.

## About the Walk

The walk starts at the car park and picnic area on Wirksworth Dale, Brassington.

The majority of Brassington village is within a conservation area, containing numerous listed structures and buildings from the 17th century and earlier.

Our walk passes many abandoned lead mines, one of which was known as Nickalum. Little evidence of the former industrial activity remains on the surface, but the remains of the mine's belland yard, built to keep grazing stock away from poisonous spoil heaps, can still be seen.

As we approach Carsington we are presented with beautiful views over Carsington Water. The reservoir opened in 1992 following years of planning and a catastrophic collapse of the dam wall in 1984, before the reservoir was flooded.

The village of Carsington also has conservation area status, together with its neighbour Hopton. Both villages contain a number of listed structures and buildings from the 17th century. The village green in Carsington is also home to a medieval preaching cross.

Carsington Pasture is a scheduled ancient monument due to the preservation of lead mines and medieval field systems, although the area is now home to four wind turbines with a further three in close proximity. Numerous artefacts have been discovered in the area, some of which are now preserved in Buxton Museum.

Above the village of Carsington we pass the King's Chair, a throne-shaped rock protruding from the pasture. Passing the wind farm, the base of a long-disused windmill can be seen in the middle of a field. The mill is thought to have been built in the 18th century and was out of use by the time the Ordnance Survey produced their 1887 map.

Our walk passes close to the top of what was once the steepest standard-gauge adhesion railway in the country; the Hopton Incline maintains a gradient of 1 in 14. The mighty outcrop of Harboro' Rocks dominates the landscape, together with a not insignificant industrial site; the area is noted for Neolithic and Iron Age activity, as well as clear evidence of more modern industrial archaeology. A short way beyond point 17 is the site of Longcliffe Station.

**Opposite page:** Brassington

44

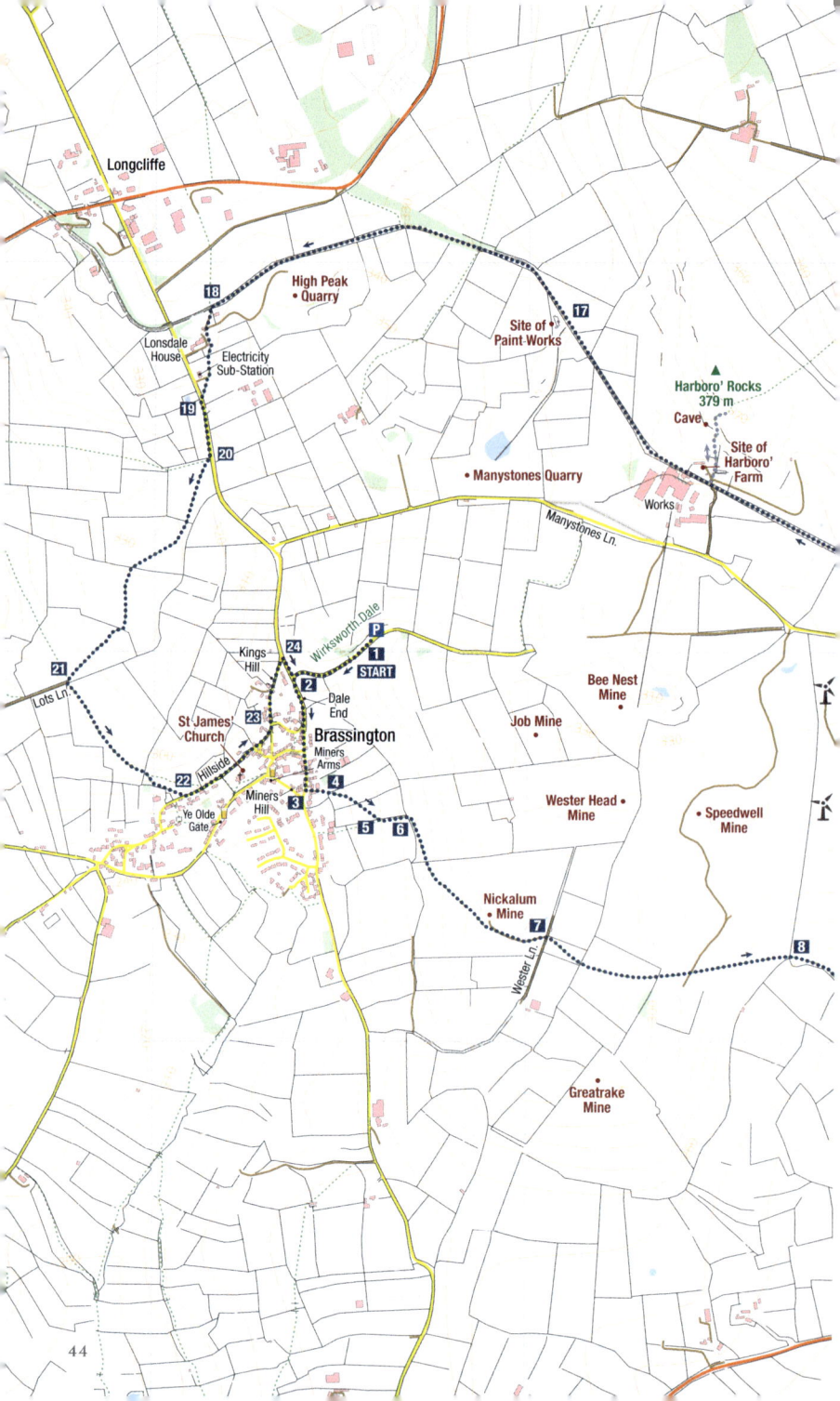

## Directions

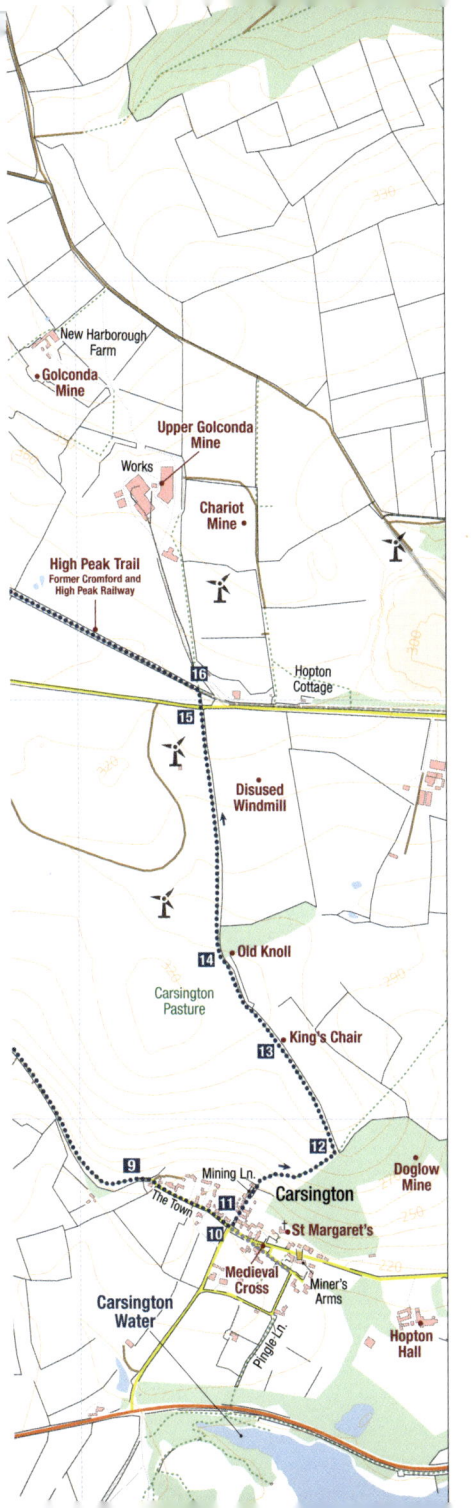

**1.** From the car park, walk down Wirksworth Dale.

**2.** Turn left into Dale End.

**3.** Opposite Miners Hill and next to Smithy Barns, follow the public footpath on your left through the farmyard. A few steps further down the road is Tudor House, with its door lintel that dates the building to 1615.

**4.** Beyond the farmyard, cross a couple of fields for around 150 yards.

**5.** After negotiating a stile, turn left to follow a wall on your left as it rises steeply and offers views back over Brassington.

**6.** Through the stile, turn right and follow the path as it passes close by the remains of Nickalum Mine; its belland yard is still visible. Beyond Nickalum Mine the path becomes a track, which you follow down to Wester Lane.

**7.** Cross Wester Lane and follow the footpath across the fields for just over a third of a mile. There is evidence of lead mining all around you and the wind turbines of Carsington Pasture on your left, and as the hill begins to fall away on your right you will see vistas over Carsington Water.

**8.** As the path descends alongside a wall to your right it becomes a more defined track. After around a third of a mile a track joins from the right from a collection of agricultural buildings.

**9.** Pass over a stile by a gate and continue along the track towards Carsington. As we walk between residential properties the track becomes metalled, now known as "The Town".

**10.** On reaching Carsington, the Miner's Arms, St Margaret's Church and the stump of a medieval preaching cross are around 100 yards ahead of you. The cross dates from the 14th or 15th century and stands at the fork between Main Street and Bottom Lane. The church of St Margaret was constructed in 1648, the date inscribed into the sundial. The Miner's Arms, a three-storey 17th century building, is best viewed from Bottom Lane. Carsington was on the route of the Oakerthorpe and Ashbourne turnpike which passed by the front of the inn, no doubt making it an ideal place to stop for refreshments.

**11.** After exploring the village, turn right up Mining Lane and ascend the steep slope and steps up to Carsington Pasture. Follow the steep grassy footpath up the hill.

**12.** Prior to the wall, turn left and follow the path, keeping the wall on your right.

**13.** After around 300 yards we pass the King's Chair on the far side of the wall.

**14.** After a further 250 yards, beside Old Knoll and with the nearest wind turbine directly in front of you, the path turns to the right heading for Brassington Lane. In the middle of the field on your right is the stone base of a windmill, which was used as a chicken house in the 1950s.

**15.** Cross Brassington Lane and join the High Peak Trail.

**16.** Turn left along the trail towards Longcliffe, continuing for around a mile and a half. During this part of the journey you will pass a factory on your left, Harboro' Rocks, caves, a cairn and the remains of former mining activity

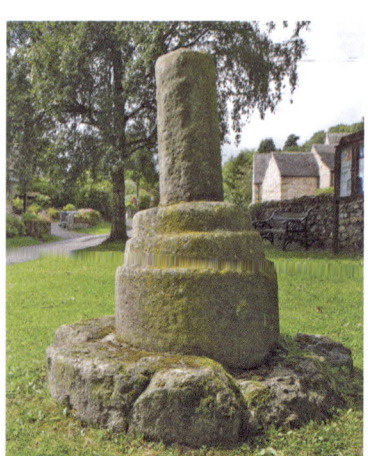

**Above left:** Medieval cross in Carsington village   **Above right:** The King's Chair, Carsington Pasture

**Above:** Harboro' Rocks

on your right. Evidence of an Iron Age settlement has been documented; some artefacts from the cave and settlement are held by Derby Museum.

**17.** Continuing along the trail you pass the site of a paint works and tramways which served Manystones Quarry, a couple of fields away to your left. Beyond the first cutting, on your left is High Peak Quarry.

**18.** After the second cutting, take the path on your left signed 'Brassington ¾ mile', following a new fence line and passing behind Lonsdale House and an electricity substation.

**19.** Turn left onto the Brassington road and continue for around 150 yards.

**20.** Turn right across the fields along a waymarked path signed 'Limestone Way' and Ballidon.

**21.** After around half a mile the path becomes a walled track, Lotts Lane. Do not follow the track; instead turn left across the fields towards Brassington.

**22.** Turn left onto Hillside. The 12th century church of St James clings to the hillside below to your right.

**23.** Keep left and continue up Kings Hill, before descending once more to Dale End.

**24.** Turn right down Dale End, and after a few yards turn left into Wirksworth Dale, arriving back at your starting point.

On the High Peak Trail looking towards Minninglow

# Walk 8: Minninglow and Roystone Grange

## Essential Information

**Start:** Minninglow Car Park, Mouldridge Lane, near Pikehall.

**Public Transport:** There is no public transport within close proximity to this route.

**Facilities:** There are no facilities close to the route.

**Car Park:** A small, free car park at Gotham, signed Minninglow car park, is adjacent to the High Peak Trail.

**Distance:** 6 miles

## About the Walk

Our walk commences at Minninglow car park, near Gotham. We follow the High Peak Trail around the incredibly tight Gotham curve and Minninglow embankment. Evidence of the area's industrial past can be seen at Minninglow, where there are the remains of a crane and lime kiln.

Skirting the ancient burial site and prominent hilltop feature of Minninglow itself, accessible via a concessionary path as an optional diversion, we descend towards Roystone Grange and pass a former engine house, which provided compressed air to the local quarries. Passing between Hoe Grange Quarry and Ballidon Quarry, we return via Lowmoor Farm and Gotham.

WALK 8: MINNINGLOW AND ROYSTONE GRANGE

## Directions

**1.** From the car park, cross Mouldridge Lane and follow the High Peak Trail towards Minninglow.

**2.** After just shy of a mile, you will reach the site of a former quarry on your left. The rusting, skeletal remains of a crane indicate where minerals were once loaded onto the waiting wagons of the Cromford and High Peak Railway.

If you wish, on your left and just beyond the remnants of the crane there is a concessionary path to Minninglow. Ascend the rocky field into the ancient site, following the path out through the far side of the enclosure, turning right and downhill back towards the High Peak Trail. You will rejoin the main route at point 4. Otherwise, continue along the trail, crossing the embankment, with an old lime kiln visible ahead and to the left.

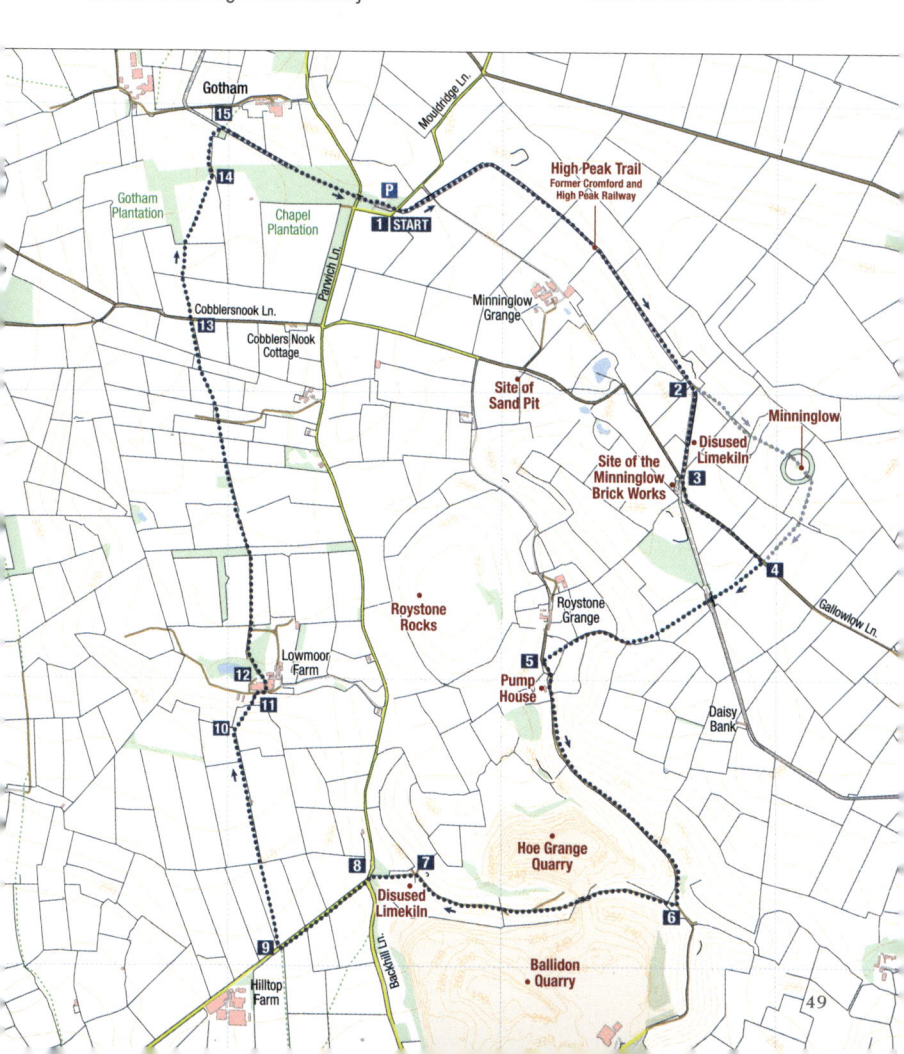

**Above:** Remains of a crane on the High Peak Trail

**Opposite page left:** Minninglow **Right:** The Pump House near Roystone Grange

**3.** At the site of Minninglow Brick Works, turn left along Gallowlow Lane with Minninglow above and to your left, continuing for a couple of hundred yards. Little remains of the brick works, which was to the right of the High Peak Trail where Gallowlow Lane crossed, and which once had a tramway descending to the clay and sand pits below. Gallowlow Lane was part of the network of packhorse ways and salt roads that once crossed Derbyshire.

**4.** Take the footpath on your right (straight ahead if coming from Minninglow), which crosses a stile and takes you under the High Peak Trail. Continue ahead and downhill to Roystone Grange. Roystone Grange farmhouse dates from the late 18th century, but occupation of the site as a monastic grange dates from the 13th century when the land was given to Garendon Abbey in Leicestershire by Adam de Herthill.

**5.** At the lane turn left, passing the Pump House on your right and descending into the dale for around three quarters of a mile towards Ballidon. The Pump House once generated compressed air for use by machinery in the nearby quarries.

**6.** Where the lane bears left, turn right through a gate and walk along a lane between two spits of land. You are passing between Hoe Grange and Ballidon quarries; you will cross a bridge over a roadway between the two.

**7.** At the remains of a lime kiln, keep left, making your way uphill to Parwich Lane.

**8.** At Parwich Lane, turn left and then immediately right, following the unnamed road for around a quarter of a mile.

**9.** Turn right over a stile and cross fields to Lowmoor Farm, passing a barn on your right. Head for a stile below the barn.

# WALK 8: MINNINGLOW AND ROYSTONE GRANGE

**10.** The path to Lowmoor Farm follows the wall line, crosses a stile and descends steeply to the farmyard.

**11.** Pass around the left-hand side of the cowshed facing you and follow the signed path through the farmyard. Look for a stile in the wall ahead, and cross it to reach a lane.

**12.** Turn left to follow the lane uphill, through the trees and into fields. Follow the path for around three quarters of a mile; take the left-hand gate where the path splits, and cross numerous dilapidated stone walls to reach Cobblersnook Lane. Cobblersnook Lane formed part of the same packhorse way as Gallowlow Lane.

**13.** Cross Cobblersnook Lane, heading for a gap in the trees ahead of you at one o'clock. The path initially heads away from the destination of this instruction by virtue of following a field boundary that has long since disappeared; cross a stile to the left of a gate in the first wall, and then bear right to another stile, clipping the edge of the woodland as you turn to head towards the gap between Gotham and Chapel Plantations.

**14.** Negotiate the earthen track between the plantations before following the path and the wall line back downhill to the High Peak Trail, with Gotham Granges in front of you.

**15.** Turn right along the trail and follow it back to the Minninglow car park.

*The High Peak Trail*

# Walk 9: Minninglow, Pikehall and Aleck Low

## Essential Information

**Start:** Minninglow Car Park, Mouldridge Lane, near Pikehall.

**Public Transport:** There is no public transport within close proximity to this route.

**Facilities:** There are no facilities close to the route.

**Car Park:** A small, free car park at Gotham, signed Minninglow car park, is adjacent to the High Peak Trail.

**Distance:** 4¾ miles

## About the Walk

From the car park we walk alongside the impressive limestone Minninglow embankment before turning into Hedge Lane. Hedge Lane was part of the Roman road known as The Street, linking Buxton (Aquae Arnemetiae) with Derby (Derventio).

At Pikehall we turn back towards the trail, making our way past the ancient burial ground of Aleck Low. We return to Minninglow car park via the well trodden former packhorse way known as Cardlemere Lane and past Gotham Grange farm.

WALK 9: MINNINGLOW, PIKEHALL AND ALECK LOW

## Directions

**1.** From Minninglow car park, turn left onto Mouldridge Lane. Follow the lane for a little under half a mile as it descends alongside the Minninglow embankment.

**2.** Turn left into Hedge Lane, which follows the alignment of the Roman, Buxton (Aquae Arnemetiae) to Derby (Derventio) road, and the later Derby Lane.

**3.** At Pikehall, turn left onto the busy Newhaven road for around 150 yards. Ogilby's map of c1675 indicates that Pikehall was home to the Pikeham Inn.

**4.** Turn left into Parwich Lane and then right onto Green Lane. Follow Green Lane to the High Peak Trail.

**5.** Turn right onto the High Peak Trail and follow it for around a quarter of a mile.

**6.** Take the lane on your left and follow it for approximately 150 yards.

**7.** Cross the stile on your right and follow the path for a mile, crossing several field boundaries to reach the Buxton-to-Ashbourne road (A515). As you reach the crest of the hill, to your right is Aleck Low, a bowl barrow dating from the Late Neolithic to Late Bronze Age period (2400 to 1500 BCE). It was excavated by Thomas Bateman in 1843.

**8.** Turn left onto the A515, and then immediately left into Cardlemere Lane. Follow the lane for approximately half a mile. Cardlemere Lane is an ancient trackway; many of these crossed the barren uplands of Derbyshire, providing a well-trodden navigation network for travellers, traders and those in charge of packhorse trains.

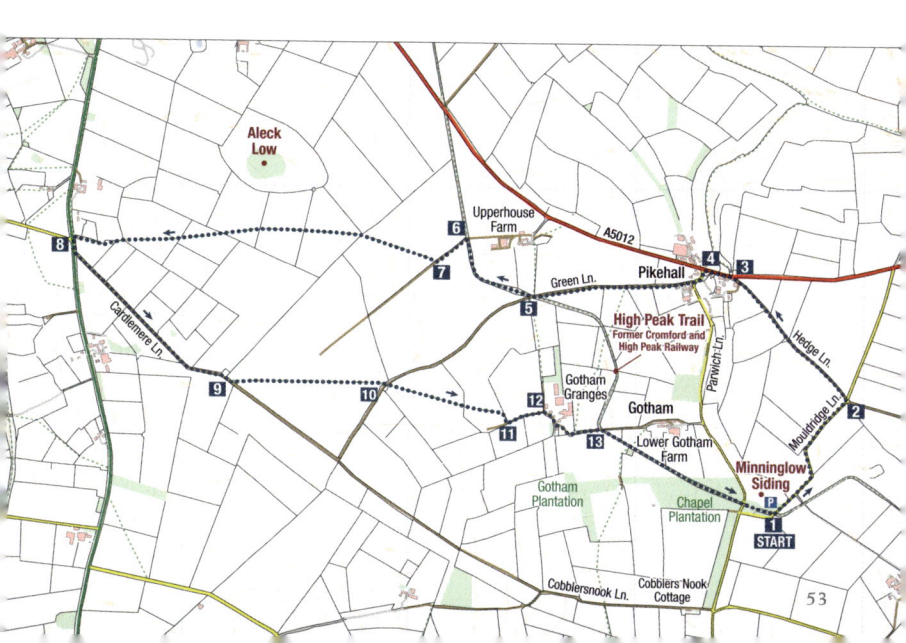

**9.** Take the footpath on your left across the field to Green Lane.

**10.** Cross Green Lane and take the path towards Gotham Grange.

**11.** Turn left into the lane to the Gotham Grange farmyard.

**12.** Follow the path through the farmyard to the right, and then take the lane to the left down to the High Peak Trail. The path through Gotham Grange farmyard is signposted and stiles are provided at all gates within the yard.

**13.** Turn right onto the High Peak Trail, following it back to the Minninglow car park.

**Above:** The prominent landmark of Minninglow sits above Gotham limestone embankment

# Walk 10: Friden, Pikehall and the Dales

> **Essential Information**
>
> **Start:** Friden Car Park, near Newhaven.
>
> **Public Transport:** There is no public transport within close proximity to this route.
>
> **Facilities:** There are no facilities on or close to the route.
>
> **Car Park:** A small, free car park at Friden is adjacent to the High Peak Trail.
>
> **Distance:** 6 miles

## About the Walk

This walk takes us from the car park at Friden along the High Peak Trail to near Minninglow, and then to Pikehall and down into the Long Dale National Nature Reserve.

The route twice crosses the busy A5012 Newhaven-to-Cromford road, known locally as the Via Gellia after the prosperous Gell family of industrialists. Prior to this section of the road being maintained by the Cromford to Newhaven Turnpike Trust it was the responsibility of the Nottingham to Newhaven Turnpike Trust. There is also a section of the walk along the Newhaven-to-Bakewell road, which has no pavement. Extreme caution should be exercised at these points.

The course of the Roman road The Street is both walked along and crossed during this walk. The later Derby Lane followed a similar route in this area, and it too is utilised.

This is a lead-mining area. While the mines are capped, you should not walk in any of the many depressions left by mining activity.

Friden, the site of a silica fire brickworks dating from 1892, continues in the production of refractory products. There were a number of level crossings along this stretch of the railway line, the most notable being the one that crosses the A5012. The Minninglow car park near Gotham occupies the site of the old Minninglow sidings.

Pikehall is a hamlet containing structures dating from the 18th century. Both Gratton Dale and Long Dale offer a wealth of fauna and flora, with Long Dale being a National Nature Reserve.

## Directions

**1.** From the car park at Friden, face the trail and turn right to follow it for just over three quarters of a mile in a south-easterly direction, signposted for Minninglow, Middleton Top and High Peak Junction.

**2.** Follow the trail over the busy A5012 at the Newhaven Crossing to reach Minninglow car park after a mile and a half.

**3.** Turn left onto Mouldridge Lane, descending alongside the limestone embankment of the High Peak Trail, and follow the lane as it rises for around half a mile.

**4.** Turn left into Hedge Lane, following it to its end at Pikehall. Hedge Lane is one of Derbyshire's ancient trackways; both the Roman road The Street and the later Derby Lane passed this way on a similar alignment. If you look ahead, through Pikehall Farm and up the hill, that is the direction the old roads took.

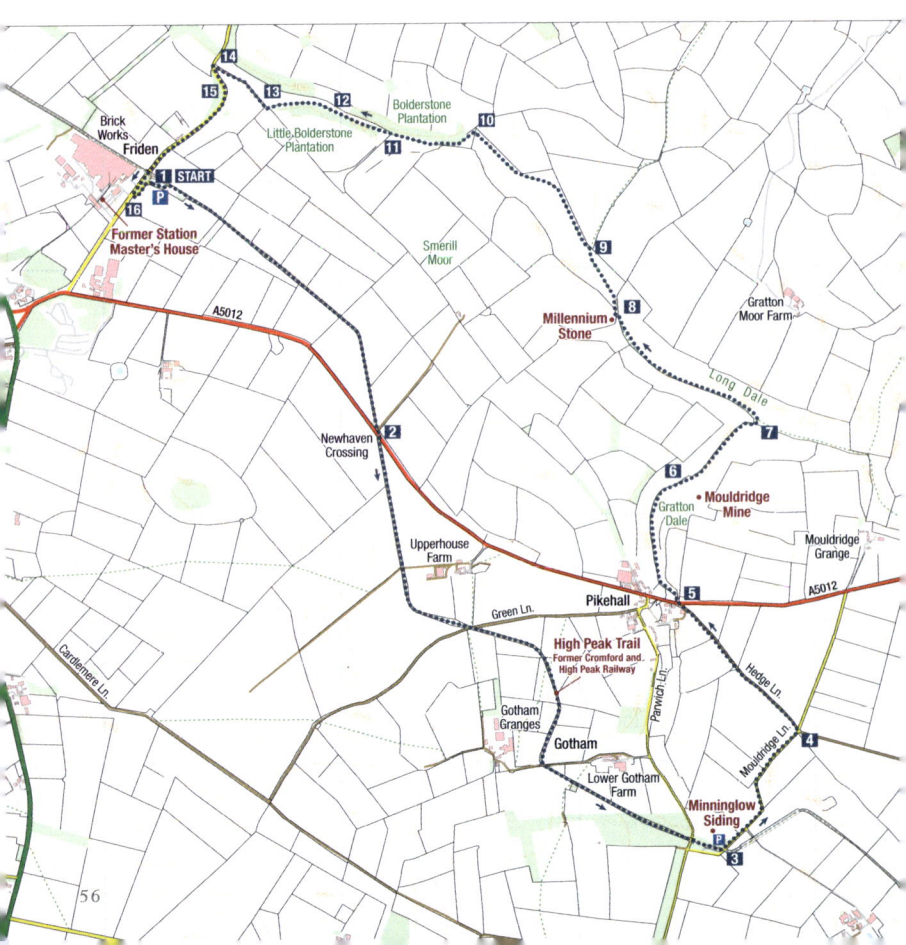

WALK 10: FRIDEN, PIKEHALL AND THE DALES

Long Dale

**5.** At Pikehall re-cross the busy A5012 and pass through two pedestrian gates. Follow the path down Gratton Dale.

**6.** Pass the entrance to Mouldridge Mine on your right and continue to descend.

**7.** Gratton Dale meets Long Dale, where you need to pass through the gate and turn left along the wide grassy path, keeping to the valley bottom.

**8.** Go through the gate in the wall adjacent to the 'Markerstones for the Millennium' installation on your left. Follow the path uphill.

**9.** At the wall line, do not go through the gate ahead; instead, take the left-hand path.

**10.** Continue through the gate into a field which skirts the edge of Boulderstone Plantation, keeping the boundary to the woodland on your right.

**11.** With a wall in front of you, climb the stile and follow the left-hand edge of the field.

**12.** Join a narrow walled trackway running close under the conifers on the left-hand boundary of the field.

**13.** Follow the lane's course as it turns to the right. This is the area in which we cross the probable alignment of The Street and Derby Lane.

**14.** At the end of the track, continue through the gate, turning left and rising up to the road.

**15.** Continue uphill towards Friden, passing under the bridge carrying the High Peak Trail. The Station Master's house is on your right, almost opposite the drive to the High Peak Trail car park.

**16.** Turn left onto the High Peak Trail to reach the Friden car park.

## Long Dale Nature Reserve

This dry valley is home to a wide variety of flora and fauna during the late spring and summer months, making this the ideal time to plan your visit. The pinks of orchids contrast with the bright yellows of cowslips, supporting less common butterfly species such as the dark green fritillary. Because it is inaccessible by motor vehicle this valley has remained relatively unspoiled. However, the adjoining Gratton Dale contains Mouldridge Mine, the spoil from which has created an ideal habitat for alpine pennycress and leadwort (spring sandwort).

**Opposite page:** The restored signal box at Hartington Station on the Tissington Trail

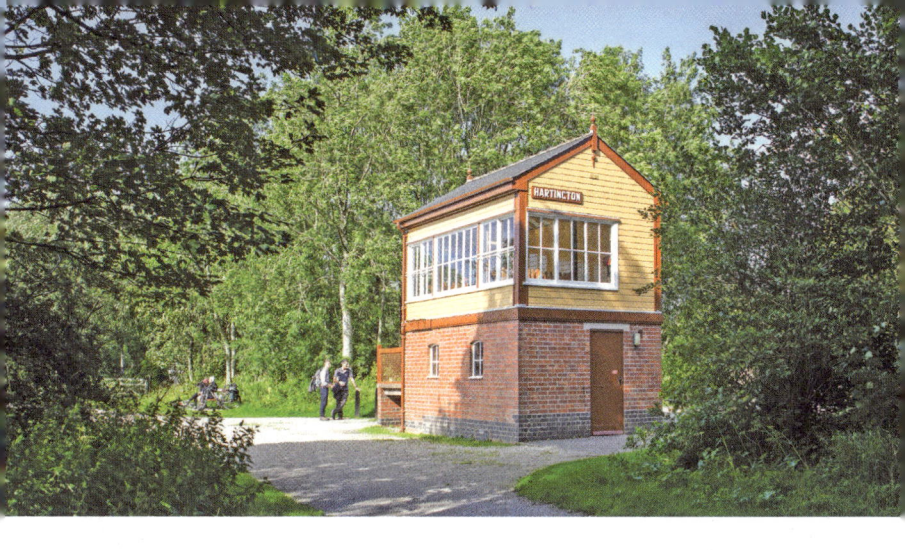

# Walk 11: Parsley Hay and Hartington Station

## Essential Information

**Start:** Parsley Hay Bike Hire Centre, off the A515 Buxton to Ashbourne Road.

**Public Transport:** Bus: Parsley Hay is served by the very infrequent 441, which runs Monday to Saturday once a day in each direction between Ashbourne and Buxton.

**Facilities:** Parsley Hay offers a shop selling light refreshments, toilets and a cycle hire centre. Hartington Station has toilets, and a refreshments van may be available at peak times.

**Car Park:** There are pay and display car parks at Parsley Hay and Hartington Station.

**Distance:** 5 miles

## About the Walk

This walk takes us from Parsley Hay visitor centre to Hartington Station, with its preserved signal box, via the Tissington Trail. We then go cross-country, passing Hartington Pasture Nature Reserve to rejoin the High Peak Trail before returning to Parsley Hay.

**Note**: This walk crosses the wide and busy A515, the main Ashbourne-to-Buxton road, with fast-moving traffic.

**Above:** Parsley Hay in the snow, c.1960s contrasted with a present-day view from the same location

## Directions

**1.** With your back to Parsley Hay visitor centre, turn left to head south along the High Peak Trail.

**2.** At the former junction between the Cromford and High Peak Railway and the Ashbourne branch of the LNER, take the right-hand fork along the Tissington Trail signposted for Hartington and Ashbourne. Continue along the trail for just over a mile and a half to Hartington Station. Beyond Parsley Hay cutting, on your right was the site of the High Peak Silica Company sidings.

**3.** A few yards beyond Hartington Station, take the footpath and steps on your left to walk up the embankment. Hartshead Quarry is on your right and Station Quarry on your left. The path forks after around quarter of a mile, with the right-hand path leading to Hartington Meadows Nature Reserve.

**4.** Take the left-hand fork uphill and then down again to the B5054 Hartington road.

**5.** Turn left down the road for a few yards.

**6.** Turn right onto a green lane, following it uphill to the A515 Ashbourne-to-Buxton road.

**7.** Cross the busy A515 and continue along Green Lane until you reach the High Peak Trail.

**8.** Turn left along the High Peak Trail, reaching the short Newhaven Tunnel in just under a mile. Along this stretch of the trail survive both the original stone mile markers and the more modern concrete replacements, gradient posts, and the distant signal post that once protected Parsley Hay junction. Both ends of Newhaven Tunnel are adorned with carved stones, one dedicated to the Cromford and High Peak Railway 1825 and the other to the engineer Josias Jessop.

**9.** Carry on along the trail to Parsley Hay junction and onward to return to the visitor centre.

61

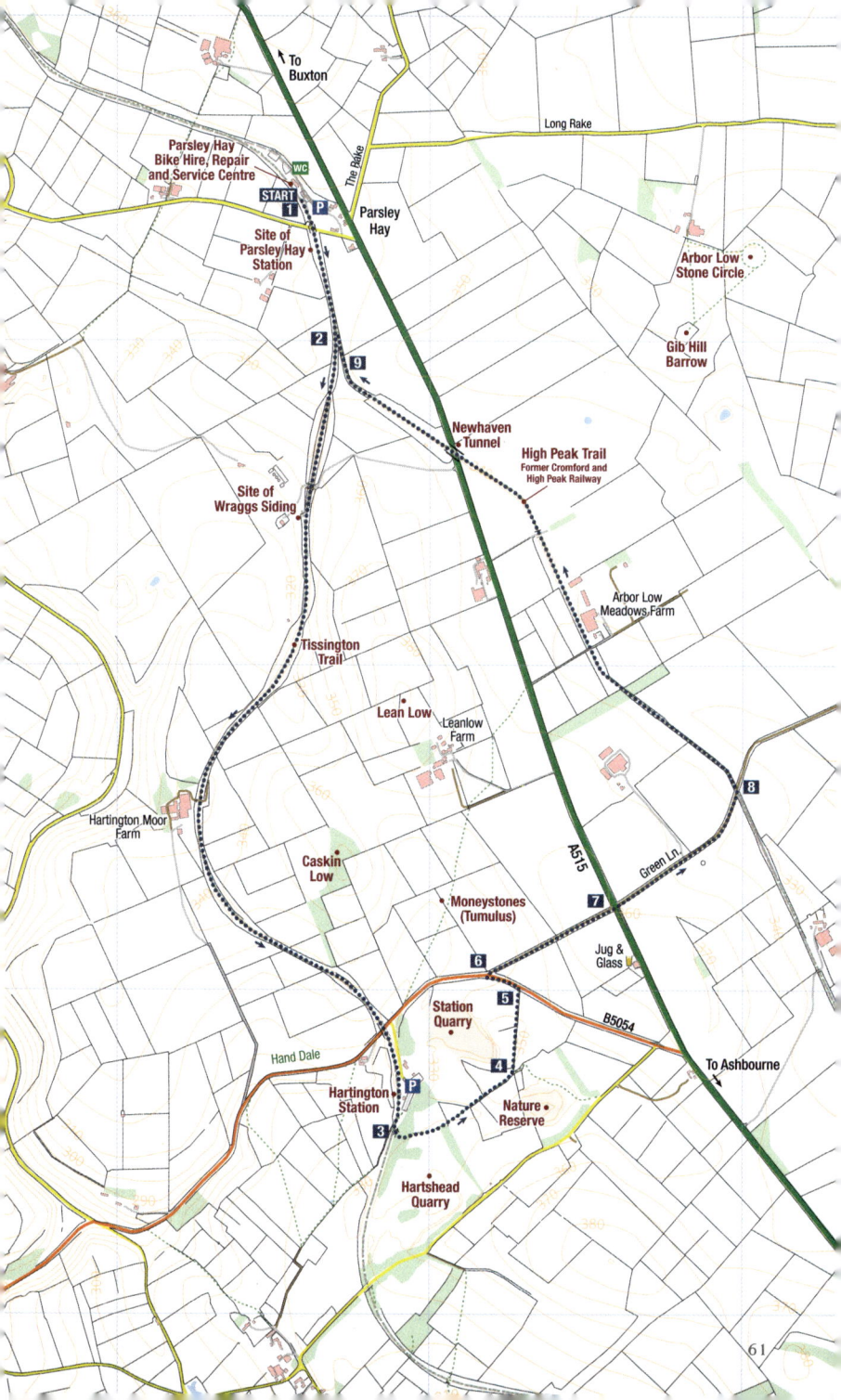

# Walk 12: Sparklow, Flagg and Pomeroy

## Essential Information

**Start:** Hurdlow Station Car Park, 7 miles south of Buxton, off the A515 Buxton to Ashbourne Road.

**Public Transport:** Bus: Pomeroy and the Bull i Thorn are served by the very infrequent route 441, which runs once a day in each direction, Monday to Saturday, between Ashbourne and Buxton. Service 58, which operates twice a day between Chatsworth House and Macclesfield on Sundays and Bank Holidays, stops at Pomeroy and the Bull i Thorn, and also at the junction of Tagg Lane and the A515, close to Sparklow.

**Facilities:** The Royal Oak at Sparklow, the Bull i Thorn café and the Duke of York pub all offer refreshments on or very close to this route.

**Car Park:** Hurdlow Station car park is operated by the Peak District National Park (fees apply).

**Distance:** 5 miles

## About the Walk

This walk takes us from Hurdlow Station at Sparklow towards Flagg. We cross the course of the Roman Road called The Street at Bull i Thorn, then follow Hutmoor Butts, a green lane which takes us to a restored barn close to a site that was once a hive of industrial activity, busy with lead mines and associated works. After a short stretch along a quiet lane we return to the fields heading for Pomeroy, crossing the line of The Street once more and passing Street Farm with Street House Farm not far away, these names reflecting the name of the highway on which this community grew. We cross the High Peak/Tissington trail to reach the shrunken medieval settlement of Hurdlow Town, with its grade II listed hall and manor, where the original course of the Cromford and High Peak Railway can clearly be seen. We return to Hurdlow Station via the High Peak Trail, passing the foot of the Hurdlow Incline which saw its last working on 2nd January 1869.

**Note:** Twice during this walk we cross the wide and busy A515, with fast-moving traffic in both directions.

WALK 12: SPARKLOW, FLAGG AND POMEROY

Duke of York, Pomeroy

## Directions

**1.** From the car park at Hurdlow Station, head north-west along the High Peak Trail, passing under the Tagg Lane road bridge.

**2.** A short distance beyond the bridge and the site of Hurdlow Station, take the path that diverges to the right to follow the boundary wall of the trail.

**3.** At the gate beside the bridge under the trail, turn right and follow the path as it ascends the hill, crossing the route of The Street shortly before arriving at the A515 and the former Bull i' th' Thorn pub, now the Bull i Thorn café.

**4.** Cross the busy A515 Buxton-to-Ashbourne road, and turn right.

**5.** After only a few yards, turn left to walk down Hutmoor Butts track, passing the Derbyshire Donkey Sanctuary on your right.

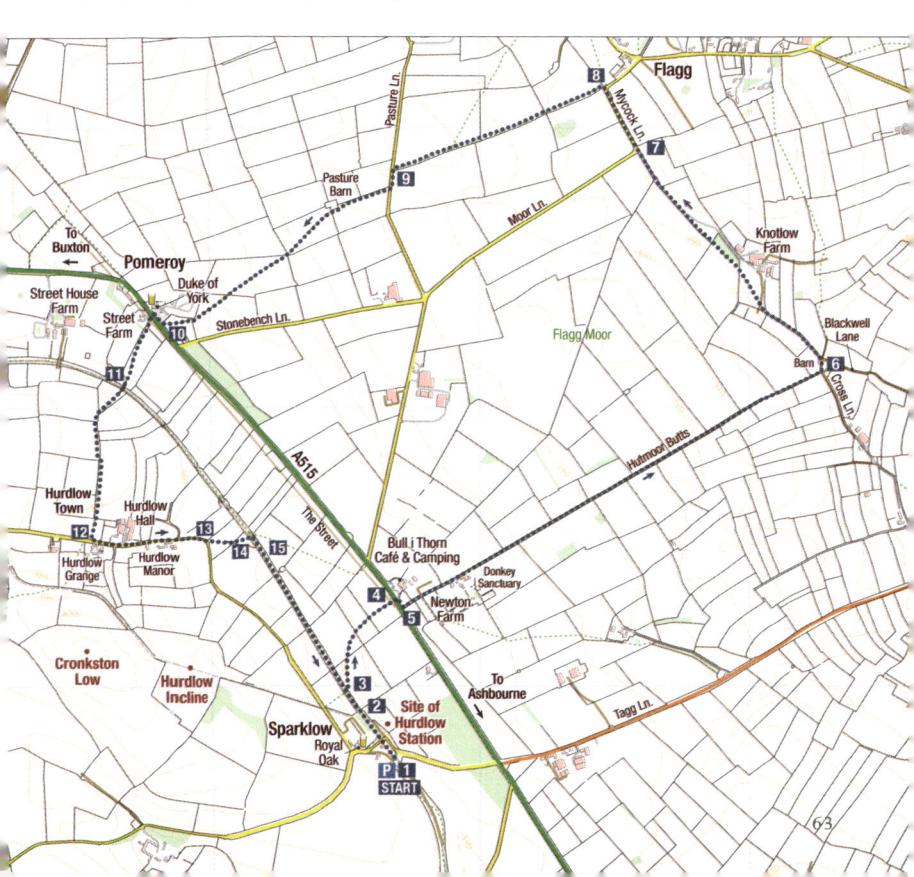

Hurdlow Grange

**6.** Follow Hutmoor Butts to its end at the junction with Cross Lane and Blackwell Lane. Turn left at the barn and take the leftmost path waymarked 'Limestone Way', passing Knotlow Farm down the hillside to your right.

**7.** Where the path becomes Mycock Lane, keep straight ahead until the road makes a sharp turn to the right.

**8.** Here you should pass through the gate ahead of you, taking the footpath immediately on your left over the fields towards Pasture Lane.

**9.** At Pasture Lane, turn left and after a few yards turn right over the fields towards Pasture Barn, although no buildings now exist at this location. Continue to the Duke of York at Pomeroy.

**10.** At the Duke of York, re-cross the busy A515 and take the path towards Hurdlow Town.

**11.** Cross the bridge over the High Peak/Tissington Trail, continuing towards the shrunken medieval settlement of Hurdlow Town, which now consists of three farms. Looking over the fields to the right of Hurdlow Grange you will see the original course of the Cromford and High Peak Railway, with a bridge still standing.

**12.** Opposite Hurdlow Grange, turn left down the lane towards Sparklow.

**13.** After around 400 yards, after a right-hand bend, take the footpath left across the fields towards the bridge under the High Peak Trail.

**14.** Pass under the bridge and cross the stile immediately on your right, ascending steps up onto the trail.

**15.** Turn left on the trail and make your way back to Hurdlow Station, around half a mile away.